The USE of ECONOMIC INSTRUMENTS in ENVIRONMENTAL POLICY: OPPORTUNITIES and CHALLENGES

UNEP/ETB/2003/9

UNITED NATIONS PUBLICATION

ISBN: 92-807-2391-X

Printed on paper from 100 % recycled waste material
CyclusOffset

Designed and printed by TYPHON - Annecy
00 33 (0)4 50 10 00 00

JUL 2 7 2004

Foreword

As natural resources come under increasing pressure around the world, national governments, international agencies, communities and businesses are increasingly called upon to address environmental problems. However, continual budget constraints and institutional weaknesses often make it difficult to achieve the necessary levels of environmental protection.

Economic instruments make use of market mechanisms and provide one important approach to address this challenge. They encompass a broad array of policy tools, ranging from pollution taxes and marketable permits to deposit-refund systems and performance bonds. Economic instruments are applied across a similarly wide-ranging set of policy sectors, including land, water and air management, and control or reduction of pollutants. They either drive up the cost of environmentally harmful activities or increase the returns from sustainable approaches, thereby creating economic incentives to behave in a more environmentally responsible and sustainable manner.

By their nature, economic instruments can increase efficiency by allowing polluters greater flexibility in deciding how and when to meet their targets, while encouraging the design of new and improved abatement technologies. Economic instruments can also lower regulatory expenditures, as less monitoring and surveillance is often required. In addition, some economic instruments will actually raise revenue for governments, providing an important source of finance for sectors of priority in the country.

The challenge frequently heard from policy makers and experts, however, is how to move from the theory of using economic instruments to their practical application: how to choose the appropriate tools and integrate them effectively with a pre-existing regulatory structure.

This report seeks to help policy makers, especially in the developing world, to identify, evaluate and apply economic instruments to address a country's environmental problems within its national and local circumstances. It presents an innovative approach by offering tools for a comprehensive assessment of the country context and conditions and by tailoring solutions to the specific country needs. The report also provides practical guidance on identifying when economic instruments may be most appropriate, and on strengthening the support framework needed to introduce them.

I hope that policy makers find this report a useful tool and that it will assist them to make increased use of economic instruments for environmental policy and sustainable development. UNEP welcomes comments and feedback on this report.

Klaus Töpfer
Executive Director
United Nations Environment Programme

1

Executive Summary

Threats to human health and environmental quality continue to grow worldwide. Patterns of industrial production, as well as the use of natural and land resources, are important contributing factors. While environmental problems vary in their details, they generally involve either overuse of a natural resource or emission of damaging pollutants. Transitioning to more sustainable use patterns is both difficult and expensive even under optimum conditions. Developing countries face the added challenges of severe funding constraints, weak institutional capacity, and a dependence on environmental and natural resources for economic development.

Policy options to address these problems fall into two general categories: command and control (CACs) and market-based economic instruments (EIs). EIs encompass a range of policy tools from pollution taxes and marketable permits to deposit-refund systems and performance bonds. The common element of all EIs is that they operate on a decentralized level through their impact on market signals. Under most scenarios, they shift the costs and responsibilities associated with pollution back on to the polluter more efficiently than do CACs, which rely on mandated technologies and/or pollution reduction targets applied universally across polluters. Although the policy approaches differ and are often contrasted against each other, in reality the two often operate alongside each other. Governments may, for example, mandate caps on allowable pollution for a region or country and use market-oriented approaches such as tradable permits to allocate the allowable emissions in an efficient manner.

A combination of factors seems to explain the current dominance of CAC approaches throughout the world despite the benefits of EIs. These include: a lack of understanding of how EIs work to protect the environment and how to choose the appropriate instrument; political interests that seek to minimize control costs via regulation; and a preference for keeping the status quo. Opportunities for much greater environmental and economic gains are therefore lost.

This report aims to provide policy makers, especially in developing countries, with practical guidance on deciding which types of EIs are likely to work in addressing specific environmental problems. It describes how EIs modify incentives to pollute, the process of introducing EIs into the existing policy regime, the supporting conditions needed for them to work, and the potential effects of EIs on important societal factors such as poverty and sustainable development. The paper also introduces a number of template-based tools to assist policy makers assemble disparate data in a more efficient and structured way. These tools will enable policy makers to refine their understanding of a particular environmental challenge, to more quickly identify appropriate policy options, and to more effectively tailor these solutions to local conditions.

Benefits of economic instruments

Economic instruments operate by realigning rights and responsibilities of firms, groups or individuals so that they have both the incentive and the power to act in a more environmentally responsible manner. Markets inherently use less of more expensive inputs, and invest more in activities that promise higher returns. EIs drive up the price of environmentally damaging inputs, as well as increase the returns to more sustainable approaches. When implemented carefully, EIs tend to reduce the societal cost to achieve any given level of environmental quality.

EIs can accomplish a number of important changes in market dynamics. First, the cost of pollution is shifted more effectively back onto polluters than with CACs. While CACs often allow emissions/resource extraction below the regulatory threshold to occur for free, EIs tend to price all units of pollution/resource use. This encourages people to use goods and services that do less environmental damage, and polluting firms to control more than required in order to sell their excess to others at a profit. EIs reduce compliance costs by allowing polluters to allocate pollution reductions more heavily where they are less expensive to achieve. EIs may also establish more secure property rights, allowing resource managers to take on a longer time horizon; or they may earn revenues that can finance the government's management of resources more effectively. Finally, many EIs require less public sector management and oversight than CACs, thus reducing costs and allowing greater success in countries that have some institutional gaps.

The greater potential efficiency of EIs, however, must be balanced against other policy constraints: policy baselines, institutional weaknesses, legal gaps, or strong opposing political factions. In achieving a workable policy mix, it is important to view EIs not as a sole solution in all circumstances, but as one component of a wider policy package, complementing rather than replacing existing CAC policies. Much of the challenge of choosing and implementing an appropriate policy solution comes in how to weave more flexible EIs into the existing policy and institutional conditions in the country.

Choosing appropriate policies

EIs have been proposed and implemented around the world to address a host of environmental concerns, from solid waste management and protecting biodiversity, to sustainable land use and reduction of air pollution. They have had varying degrees of success. EIs include policy instruments such as permits, quotas, licenses, concessions, user fees, use taxes, access fees, impact fees, performance bonds, deposits, rights to sue, and financial assurance. Taken together, EIs are structured to achieve some mix of three main objectives: establishing, clarifying or improving property rights; ensuring that resource users or polluters pay a fair price for what they consume or pollute; and subsidizing cleaner alternatives. In addition, many EIs have the benefit that they generate revenues for the public sector.

While many existing studies group EIs by the instrument type, this report categorizes them along their functional objectives. The aim is to provide a more intuitive system by which policy makers can quickly narrow the range of EI options suited to the specific environmental problem and baseline conditions in the country. Report Exhibit 2.1 illustrates the impacts of economic instruments categorized by their functional objective and elaborates on various factors that affect implementation to further delineate how to map out the surrounding policy context.

Prior to designing and applying any policy instrument for environmental protection, the policy context must be understood, including the existing institutional, legal and economic conditions in which these tools are meant to function. Choosing an effective policy package that will both address the environmental problem policy makers are faced with and fit in with the institutional capabilities and existing policy framework remains one of the most difficult challenges. In fact, country analysts have noted that often there is no formal process of evaluation at all prior to recommending a particular policy approach.

This report establishes a four-phase process to help policy makers choose an appropriate policy instrument and implement it accordingly. Phase 1 involves assembling existing information in a structured way. Creating this structure is a critical step, as it drives the process of assessing the solutions that may work from those that may not, as well as the identification of key data gaps. Phase 2 takes the general information provided by Phase 1 and uses it to develop initial policy proposals. Phase 3 brings in stakeholders for feedback on these initial options, and collects important information on how to refine them to increase their likelihood of success or to gauge any major resistance. Phase 4, the process of implementation, involves establishing from the outset a strict timeline for implementing the chosen policy package. Parallel work to ensure effective monitoring and enforcement is also essential.

To assist this process, the report introduces a template (Exhibit 3.1) to help define the problem and evaluate the baseline conditions. It suggests key questions that policy makers should ask in order to establish a clear understanding of the barriers and drivers of policy change. Initial completion of the template should be based on existing knowledge and identify information gaps. The template then becomes a guideline to the process of policy development, incorporating the views of stakeholders, and ultimately to implement the policy package. Investing the time to properly evaluate these factors can greatly enhance the quality of the policies developed, as well as their ability to address potential impacts on poverty or trade.

The final phase, policy implementation and evaluation, suggests using a simple matrix (Exhibit 3.2) to compare the final options across key policy parameters, including performance, anticipated side-effects and feasibility. The use of the matrix involves summarizing policy options and applying corresponding rankings to ensure that important data and impact categories are compared for each suitable EI option.

Policy implementation lessons

To complement the proposed guidelines, the report analyses a range of country studies to identify patterns in which instruments have worked effectively to address particular types of environmental problems. Following the structure of the report, case studies are organized according to the functional objective of the instrument applied rather than by the environmental harm addressed. For example, groupings include "limiting access to publicly owned resources" or "recovering reasonable fees from resource users" rather than "air pollution". The benefits of this approach are evident in the consistency of the patterns that emerge not only from the cases analysed in detail (write-ups included in Annex C), but also in Exhibit 4.1 that integrates the cases reviewed with data gathered from multi-country surveys of EI applications.

These patterns help illustrate when and under what conditions particular EIs have been successfully applied. Generally, understanding the structure of the problem to be solved as well as the baseline conditions, and choosing an instrument most suited to address these conditions, can greatly increase the likelihood of success. But instrument choice alone is not enough. Policies must be developed holistically, paying careful attention to exactly what behaviours are being rewarded. For example, charging premiums for existing renewable energy will do little to encourage new and more technically competent supply. Similarly, levying fees based only on the trunks of trees but not on the branches will provide an incentive to waste all but the largest part of the timber.

Monitoring and enforcement is also critical to the effectiveness of many EIs. Several case studies on fisheries indicate that without accurate information, individual transferable quotas (ITOs) may worsen depletion rather than ameliorate it. Charcoal harvesting in St. Lucia also illustrated that in stabilizing the resource base with communal tenure rights, each individual harvester is given an incentive to monitor his peers to ensure cutting regimes are properly followed. Furthermore, political considerations remain at the core of many of the policies implemented. Where political opposition is strong, even the best arguments for controls, user fees, or new requirements will be heavily challenged. Involving stakeholders early and including political strategies in the design and implementation of policy to confront opposition is therefore essential.

Because the potential benefits of EIs in terms of efficiency and long-term environmental improvement can be substantial, they merit careful consideration for new policy development or reforms of existing approaches. EIs can add flexibility, precision, and dynamism to policy packages and address a wide range of environmental problems. Rights to sue, creation of tradable permits, and granting of property rights to subsistence populations can all serve to provide a decentralized, non-governmental enforcement mechanism to ensure environmental responsibilities are upheld, a great help in countries with severely limited enforcement budgets.

Ultimately, choosing the most appropriate policy is influenced by a range of factors that include environmental laws already in place, the power and technical capability of ministries involved, and the broad economic conditions within the country. It is therefore important to recognize that there is no precise formula for deciding when to apply a particular EI. However, certain patterns as to when and under what conditions EIs have been successfully employed are evident from the case reviews and analysis provided.

For instance, rights-oriented approaches can work well in these situations of overuse of natural resources by local users. They provide direct incentives to manage the resource for the long-term, while protecting jobs. Where subsistence use patterns have been long-lived, modifying land tenure to formalize rights can help achieve this balance. If consumption must be curbed, buy-out or phase-out of the existing de facto rights is a possibility. For all of these approaches, accurate and empowered monitoring and enforcement functions are needed.

Where emissions result from many different industrial pollution sources, there are likely to be widely varying costs to abate the pollution. There could be large efficiency gains from introducing pollution taxes, fees, or tradable permits. Few producers and similar technologies, however suggest minor gains from emissions trading, with potentially large oversight costs to create a market. In this situation, CAC regulatory approaches may be the more efficient option.

Where regulators have a good sense of the point at which emissions cause health problems or ecosystems begin to fray, tradable permits are often the best choice. Caps can be set in advance, either based on absolute values (e.g., tons of salmon that can be caught) or on relative values (e.g., percent of total allowable catch), allowing markets to allocate the rights efficiently.

Government owned enterprises should aim to institute pricing that achieves full recovery of costs through user fees, but with a rate design that protects the poor for subsistence consumption needs. Cost recovery should not be considered an "environmental fee" as it often is, but simply a payment for services by customers. Government owned enterprises in natural resource areas often face difficult challenges in preventing corruption (large cash flows, often poor transparency) and in instituting appropriate environmental controls (government litigation against itself is uncommon). In such cases, both the fiscal and environmental well-being of the country can be served through instituting a powerful independent audit oversight and, in some cases, privatization.

Generally, it is of great importance that long-term programme support comes from within. External resources (e.g., from NGOs or international agencies) can support initial research or training. However, they should not be relied on to operate the programme, as the entire effort will be at risk when funding priorities change. Because many EIs also raise revenue through licensing fees or permit sales, such programmes have the potential to be self-sustaining.

These are of course very general policy lessons. Choosing the most appropriate policy depends on the specific circumstances, conditions and needs within the country. Altogether, the tools presented in this paper should help policy makers to structure disparate data more efficiently in order to refine their understanding of the problem they are trying to solve, to more quickly identify appropriate policy options, and to tailor these options to local conditions.

Contents

Contents

Table of Exhibits

Acknowledgements

This report was prepared for the Economics and Trade Branch of the United Nations Environment Programme (UNEP-ETB) under the auspices the UNEP Working Group on Economic Instruments. UNEP would like to thank the author of the study, Doug Koplow of Earth Track, Inc. (www.earthtrack.net), for his principal contribution towards this publication, as well as the members of the Working Group for their valuable insight and guidance.

The UNEP Working Group on Economic Instruments was created in June 2001 by Hussein Abaza, Chief UNEP-ETB, in response to the Governing Council's request to provide assistance to countries, particularly developing countries and countries with economies in transition, to develop and apply economic instruments at the national level. The Working Group consists of twenty-five developed and developing country experts from research institutions, relevant international and non-governmental organizations and governments, all of which have greatly contributed to this publication.

Case study materials and valuable feedback on draft versions of this report were particularly provided by Jean Acquatella (United Nations Economic Commission for Latin America), Jean-Philippe Barde (Organization for Economic Cooperation and Development), Nicola Borregaard (Recursos e Investigación para el Desarrollo Sustenable), Nuria Castells and Veena Jha (United Nations Conference on Trade and Development), Herminia Francisco (University of the Philippines, Los Banos College), Ulf Jaeckel (German Federal Ministry for the Environment), Markus Lehmann (Convention on Biological Diversity), Leslie Lipper (Food and Agriculture Organization), Konrad von Moltke (Dartmouth College), Adebola Okuneye (University of Agriculture, Nigeria), Theodore Panayotou (Harvard Institute for International Development), Jan Pieters (Ministry of the Environment, Netherlands), Salah El Serafy and Ronaldo Seroa da Motta (Instituto de Pesquisa Econômica Aplicada). UNEP gratefully acknowledges their valuable contribution.

UNEP would also like to thank the German Federal Ministry for the Environment, Nature Conservation and Nuclear Safety for their financial support that made the realization of this project possible.

Anja von Moltke, Economics Affairs Officer at UNEP-ETB, was responsible for managing the project, coordinating the Working Group and editing the report, supported by Andrea Smith and Colin McKee. Administrative assistance was provided by Desiree Leon and Rahila Mughal.

United Nations Environment Programme

The United Nations Environment Programme (UNEP) is the overall coordinating environmental organization of the United Nations system. Its mission is to provide leadership and encourage partnerships in caring for the environment by inspiring, informing and enabling nations and people to improve their quality of life without compromising that of future generations. In accordance with its mandate, UNEP works to observe, monitor and assess the state of the global environment, improve the scientific understanding of how environmental change occurs, and in turn, how such change can be managed by action-oriented national policies and international agreements. UNEP's capacity building work thus centers on helping countries strengthen environmental management in diverse areas that include freshwater and land resource management, the conservation and sustainable use of biodiversity, marine and coastal ecosystem management, and cleaner industrial production and eco-efficiency, among many others.

UNEP, which is headquartered in Nairobi, Kenya, marked its first 30 years of service in 2002. During this time, in partnership with a global array of collaborating organizations, UNEP has achieved major advances in the development of international environmental policy and law, environmental monitoring and assessment, and the understanding of the science of global change. This work also supports the successful development and implementation of the world's major environmental conventions. In parallel, UNEP administers several multilateral environmental agreements (MEAs) including the Vienna Convention's Montreal Protocol on Substances that Deplete the Ozone Layer, the Convention on International Trade in Endangered Species of Wild Fauna and Flora (CITES), the Basel Convention on the Control of Transboundary Movements of Hazardous Wastes and their Disposal (SBC), the Convention on Prior Informed Consent Procedure for Certain Hazardous Chemicals and Pesticides in International Trade (Rotterdam Convention, PIC) and the Cartagena Protocol on Biosafety to the Convention on Biological Diversity as well as the Stockholm Convention on Persistent Organic Pollutants (POPs).

Division of Technology, Industry and Economics

The mission of the Division of Technology, Industry and Economics (DTIE) is to encourage decision makers in government, local authorities and industry to develop and adopt policies, strategies and practices that are cleaner and safer, make efficient use of natural resources, ensure environmentally sound management of chemicals, and reduce pollution and risks for humans and the environment. In addition, it seeks to enable implementation of conventions and international agreements and encourage the internalization of environmental costs. UNEP DTIE's strategy in carrying out these objectives is to influence decision-making through partnerships with other international organizations, governmental authorities, business and industry, and non-governmental organizations; facilitate knowledge management through networks; support implementation of conventions; and work closely with UNEP regional offices. The Division, with its Director and Division Office in Paris, consists of one centre and five branches located in Paris, Geneva and Osaka.

Economics and Trade Branch

Part of DTIE, the Economics and Trade Branch (ETB) works to enhance the capacities of countries to integrate environmental considerations into development planning and macroeconomic policies, including trade policies. ETB has a particular focus on developing and transitioning economies. The work programme of the Branch consists of three main components: economics, trade and financial services. UNEP-ETB's mission in the field of environmental economics is to promote the internalization of environmental costs and enhance the use of economic instruments for environmental policy, at national, regional and international levels, including in the specific context of MEAs. The UNEP Working Group on Economic Instruments, which was created in 2001 in response to a Governing Council mandate, serves as an advisory body to UNEP-ETB's work programme on economics. It comprises twenty-five developed and developing country experts from research institutions, relevant international and non-governmental organizations, and governments. The Working Group was instrumental in the preparation of this UNEP publication as well as the UNEP publication on Economic Instruments in Biodiversity-Related Multilateral Environmental Agreements.

For more information regarding UNEP's work on EIs and subsidy reform, please contact:

Anja von Moltke
Economics and Trade Branch (ETB)
Division of Technology, Industry and Economics (DTIE)
United Nations Environment Programme (UNEP)
11-13, Chemin des Anémones
CH-1219 Châtelaine/Geneva
Tel.: (41-22) 917 81 37
Fax: (41-22) 917 80 76
E-mail: etb@unep.ch

Internet: http://www.unep.ch/etu

1. Introduction

Interest in the use of market mechanisms to achieve environmental protection has been growing over the past few years. Rather than governments stipulating the technologies that must be used to curb pollution or the maximum allowable emissions, a process known as "command and control" (CAC), economic instruments (EIs) can provide the financial incentive to act in a more environmentally responsible manner through the use of such mechanisms as marketable permits, changes to property rights, emissions or access charges, and other financial approaches to modifying behaviour. EIs have been proposed and implemented around the world to address a host of environmental concerns, from solid waste management and protecting biodiversity, to sustainable land use and reduction of air pollution, with varying degrees of success.

EIs work by internalizing environmental costs and externalities through increasing the prices that individuals and industries must pay to use resources or to emit pollutants. As resources or emissions become more expensive, consumers have strong monetary incentives to reduce resource use, either through conservation, substituting materials with a more favourable environmental profile or rationalizing consumption. Not only does this encourage reduced emissions, but the use of EIs can also be more conducive to sustainable development by reducing pressure on natural resources. Because they are generally less expensive, more flexible, and more dynamic than CAC approaches, the increased usage of EIs can offer wide-ranging benefits to the countries that use them. Solutions aim to adhere to the polluter pays principle (PPP) as closely as possible and to resist the inevitable efforts by industry groups to have their entire transition costs from policy changes shifted to the taxpayer.

EIs can often work in a complementary fashion to CACs to increase policy efficiency, and achieve environmental targets at a lower cost. More efficient policy approaches reduce the impacts of environmental controls on industry costs and competitive position relative to alternative policies. Additionally, their ability to generate technological innovation in the areas of pollution control and prevention suggest not only that control costs are likely to further decline over time, but that some of this innovation could spur the creation of new domestic industry. Capital-intensive producers of global commodities such as coal could also face economic dislocations when forced to address the damages their production causes. Policy choice must incorporate such concerns.

The purpose of this report is to provide a practical tool to policy makers that will help them decide which specific types of EIs are likely to work given the prevailing economic, political, social, institutional, and environmental circumstances in their own countries. It suggests a structure to help more rigorously define the problem to be solved, poses a number of critical questions and discusses the potential solutions and trade-offs. Policy makers should then be able to make better use of information they already have, identify key areas where there are informational gaps, and quickly focus their work on a narrow set of promising policy options.

The report also provides policy makers with context on the use of both EIs and commonly applied CAC approaches, and offers practical guidance on when EIs may be appropriate. The report then describes the process of introducing EIs into the existing environmental policy regime, the supporting conditions needed for them to work, and the potential effects of EIs on important societal factors such as poverty and sustainable development. The baseline conditions necessary for different approaches to work are examined in particular detail.

Chapter 2 provides general background information on both EI and CAC approaches to resolving environmental problems and on the context within which EIs work. Chapter 3 focuses on choosing an appropriate mechanism for environmental protection, and includes a template for assessing baseline conditions within a country or region. It provides a structure for identifying appropriate EI options as well as "flanking" measures to offset potential negative impacts of the new policies, such as impact on poverty levels and equity. Chapter 4 reviews the successes and failures in the application of EIs around the world and identifies some important lessons learned from a number of case studies. Many of the insights from the case studies led to the development of structures and tools presented in the preceding chapter. Chapter 5 provides a summary of key findings, remaining research gaps, and future opportunities to apply EIs in equitable and efficient ways.

The report includes three Annexes that provide detailed information and specific tools that can be adapted for use by policy makers to help define their objectives and put them into practice. Annex A provides a concise primer on economic instruments, including their objectives and their variations. This information provides a practical starting point for policy makers who have not worked with EIs extensively to date. Annex B presents a number of global metrics of environmental and government performance to help assess the baseline conditions in which policy makers will be operating. Annex C provides detailed information templates on a number of country case studies to demonstrate how the tools presented in the report have been used in practice.

Altogether, these tools serve to increase the effective application and use of economic instruments to achieve environmental protection in more flexible, lower cost ways, essential to developing countries where available funds are severely limited.

2. Understanding the Policy Context for Command and Control Policies and Economic Instruments

New policy solutions occur in the context of existing institutional, legal, and economic conditions. Rarely is it possible to wipe the slate clean and start again; nor would such a move necessarily be desirable. Environmental laws, for example, have been developed over many years and with great political effort. They can provide an important framework and justification for other actions, even if they are not as efficient as one might like. The greater potential efficiency of EIs must often be balanced against these existing policy constraints, and consider the relative maturity/strength of existing legal and political institutions and political factions.

EIs need not be the sole policy response but can be beneficial even as one component of a wider policy package. For example, CAC regulations are often used to set the broad parameters (e.g., total emissions, licensing requirements, etc.) under which EIs can be used to obtain a more efficient allocation of responsibility and compliance across firms. Because EIs can *complement* rather than *replace* many CAC policies, there are many potential applications for them even in countries with existing policy constraints.

Though policy elements are routinely combined to address real world problems, these elements can sometimes work at cross purposes as well as in accord. Policy instruments must therefore be combined carefully. When this is not done, administrative costs rise and impacts on environmental performance will be neutral or even negative. For example, the more rigidly CAC standards define acceptable practice at the production plant level, the smaller the benefits from any associated EI are likely to be. Similarly, governments may apply different instruments to similar industries located in different regions; or to different industries emitting the same pollutants. In either of these cases, specific polluters can face very different financial costs, skewing their competitive position and reducing the overall efficiency of the economy.[1]

This chapter explores three aspects of the policy context. Section 2.1 examines the areas of overlap between CACs and EIs, including similar environmental objectives and baseline requirements. Section 2.2 introduces the benefits of EIs, including how they achieve greater policy dynamism and efficiency. Section 2.3 presents EIs on a more disaggregated level, including the specific market functions they are trying to serve and how policy parameters can be modified to adjust to local constraints.

2.1   Policy overlap and baseline conditions for CACs and EIs

While environmental problems vary in their details, they generally involve either overuse of a natural resource or emission of damaging pollutants. The objective of environmental policy is to modify, slow, or stop resource extraction; to reduce or eliminate emissions of concern; and to shift consumption and production patterns towards greater sustainability. These objectives are the same whether the policy instrument chosen is a CAC or EI. Normally, the more severe the damage and the stronger the link between specific activities and

---

[1] Kitamori, 2002, p. 97.

environmental harm, the more rapid and extensive the policy response should be.

In addition to similar objectives, both types of policies require many of the same baseline conditions, the fundamental elements needed for functioning markets and governance in general. Without these governmental functions in place, environmental protection has a high likelihood of failure regardless of the specific instruments applied. Policy comparisons need to take baseline weaknesses into account for a fair evaluation of policy options. Decisions to forego an EI-based approach should not be made based on drawbacks that would also apply to a CAC-based solution. Similarly, to the extent that instrument choice can offset identified weaknesses in baseline conditions, this should be done.

CACs often require much more detailed information on regulated industries than would EIs, since the government must understand the details of industrial technologies in order to set standards. Because they involve fee collection or permit sales, many EIs rely more on supportive infrastructures such as functioning markets, tax, and fiscal payments systems than do CACs. CACs, on the other hand, often require more sophisticated regulatory compliance staff and in some cases, better functioning political institutions. These differences aside, the same corruptive forces that can undermine fiscal payment, tax, and legal systems are also likely to undermine the standard setting, monitoring, and enforcement functions of government needed for CAC approaches. In some cases, EIs can help substitute for weak institutions in circumstances where the parties who buy rights monitor cheating on a decentralized level - so long as sanctions can be taken against cheaters once detected. These baseline conditions are examined in more detail below.

Legal authority and efficacy

Panayotou notes "property rights and enforcement of contracts are essential for the efficient operation of markets, on which the effectiveness of economic instruments…depends".[2] These same factors are also quite important in creating a viable CAC-based regulatory system. Unfortunately, many countries have gaps both in the authority and functioning of the legal system. Gaps in legal authority are often a larger impediment to EIs than to CACs, for a country may not have established the legal basis for implementing certain EIs, even though there is sufficient existing authority to issue CAC-oriented regulations. This is a frequent problem with the institution of pollution taxes or marketable permits. In other cases, adequate statutory bases for activities may exist, yet are not sustained by common practice. Either issue creates problems. If the legal system is not capable of enforcing property rights, then using permits to curb emissions or granting access rights to indigenous people to restrict unfettered access is not feasible.

In the spectrum of economic instruments, property rights are an interesting case. They constitute a baseline condition in that general enforcement of rights is a prerequisite to the functioning of many EIs. However, they are also an EI in their own right because specifically defined property rights such as tradable permits can by themselves generate improved resource management and markets in emissions controls.

---

[2] Panayotou, 1998, p. 111. See also Annex A for a more detailed description of property rights.

Political structure and priorities

The structure and relative power of political institutions are the next baseline conditions after the basic rule of law. Without appropriate leverage to make and implement policy, environmental improvements of any type will be difficult to achieve. In a CAC arena, the institutions must be able to set and monitor appropriate standards based on technical assessments rather than purely political ones (though politics will often play some role).

Implementation of many of the EI (or CAC/EI hybrid) approaches also requires a well functioning set of political institutions. A reasonably democratic government with ministries exerting strong fiscal oversight will be needed to manage privatization effectively, to assign initial property rights fairly, to distribute transitional or targeted subsidies under an EI-based regime with reasonable equity and efficiency, or to represent the public interest against powerful factional opponents. Weak institutions would quickly render market-based instruments worthless as firms discover they can continue operating without paying taxes or buying permits. Similarly, because patterns of corruption tend to follow economic power, resource sales or licensing without institutional independence could encourage widespread corruption.

Both EI and CAC approaches also require that political institutions punish violators. Even moderately high levels of non-compliance undermine compliance by the remaining parties both psychologically and economically (as non-complying firms will have lower operating costs). The risk of corruption demonstrates how the cost of weak institutions on environmental quality can be high. Quantitative analysis of corruption indices developed in conjunction with the Environmental Sustainability Index found that environmental sustainability had the highest correlation for all of the 67 variables tested.[3] The higher the level of corruption, the lower the level of environmental sustainability.

Where natural resource industries are owned by the government rather than by the private sector, taking action by environmental ministries against the commercial activities of other branches of government can be particularly difficult. Often, national or regional policy priorities lie outside the environmental realm, and environmental agencies may not have sufficient political capital to bring about meaningful policies of any type. This lack of power will hinder all types of policy initiatives, whether CACs or EIs - either environmental controls will be toothless, or stringent CAC-based regulatory approaches will be passed into law but never enforced. In reviewing the baseline situation then, it is important to look at both the symbolic (i.e., what laws, ministries, or companies say they are doing) and the instrumental (i.e., what they are actually doing) levels. Most countries will see some disparity between the two; sometimes the disparity can be quite large.

Although EIs cannot overcome a corrupt or weak political structure, they can nevertheless help make moderately functioning governance structures work more effectively. Consider purchased credits for emitting SO_2. If emissions standards are not enforced, the firms that have purchased credits not only have wasted their own money, but face increased competition from competitors who have evaded the system. Similarly, firms that have invested to control SO_2 beyond what is required in order to sell excess permits will see the value of those credits

---

[3] Based on the correlation of the corruption index with the recently developed Environmental Sustainability Index (ESI). Marc Levy, 2001, data and research section, pp. 300-302. The Environmental Sustainability Index (ESI) was produced by a partnership of the Word Economic Forum Global Leaders for Tomorrow Environment Task Force, the Yale Center for Environmental Law and Policy, and the Center for International Earth Science Information Network (CIESIN) at Columbia University.

decline, undermining the economics of their original investments. This group of market participants share an economic interest in seeing that particular rules are enforced. They will directly monitor compliance via continued surveillance for cheaters. EIs also provide other useful information to these firms. By tracking the number of permits purchased and the price at which they are sold, firms can gauge whether all of the firms that should be purchasing permits are in fact doing so.

Fiscal norms and perverse incentives

The fiscal baseline is also important. For example, enforced payment of regular taxes must be the norm in order for pollution tax and user-fee-based systems to have any chance of success. In addition, existing fiscal distortions can affect the efficacy of environmental controls. While many of the EIs or CAC-based policies aim to reduce pollution or to slow exploitation of natural resources, there may be concurrent fiscal policies that are subsidizing emissions and resource extraction, (e.g., see section on emission fees in China, Chapter 4). Thus, identification and removal or mitigation of such "perverse" incentives should be an integral part of any policy package. Even where political factions preclude true subsidy reform, identification (and publication) of existing perverse subsidies is an important step in achieving better decisions.

Factional analysis

Just as weak government institutions can reduce the likelihood of achieving sound environmental policies, so too can the presence of well-organized opposition groups with an economic interest either in the status quo, or in a specific pathway for the projected change. Evaluation of which groups are most powerful, and what their primary goal is should take place. Allocation of rights in the baseline is also quite important: groups with existing rights, whether actual or implied, will often have more power/interest in fighting changes to existing policies. The factional analysis should also assess what options exist for buffering any social impacts that may occur from the policy reform, especially those that affect the poor.

2.2   Benefits of EIs

EIs and CACs require many of the same baseline institutions and target the same reductions in environmental harm. Both approaches also attempt to shift the costs and responsibilities associated with pollution back onto the polluter (PPP). By forcing these costs into the production expenses of the groups causing the environmental damage, the polluter will be forced by competitive pressures to address the societally-damaging aspects of its activities. However, differences between the policy types are extremely important in terms of how successful they are in achieving their environmental targets and at what cost.

Empirical studies in the United States (US) show that the efficiency gains associated with using EIs rather than CACs have been substantial. Tietenberg suggests that CAC approaches to regulate air pollution were as much as 22 times as expensive as the least-cost, market-oriented (EI) alternative.[4] For the eleven applications studied, CAC approaches were on average six times as expensive. Anderson et al. estimated that as of 1992, EIs for air, water, and land pollution within the US had saved more than US$ 11 billion relative to a CAC baseline.[5] Assessments of EIs in multiple countries by OECD also form strong evidence of

---

[4] In Hahn, 1999.
[5] Ibid. p. 7.

cost savings.[6] These cost savings have an important corollary as well: for a given environmental budget, EIs can buy more environmental protection than can CACs. This advantage rises over time, as the dynamic attributes of EIs, such as encouraging greater investments into new control technologies, bring down the unit cost of control.

Where do these savings come from? As shown below, the more voluntary nature of EIs allows greater flexibility for firms to allocate the timing and magnitude of controls to those for whom abatement is least expensive. Improved incentives for monitoring the compliance of others, and for investing in and testing new control technologies both suggest that compliance costs will continue to fall over time, making higher levels of environmental protection more affordable. Benefits of EIs include:

- **Reduction in overall cost of achieving emission reductions by providing flexibility**
  Rather than forcing every firm to meet a specific emissions level, EIs often ensure that the overall economy hits a particular level, but allow the markets to determine which specific firms control how much pollution. This encourages industries where emissions reductions are less costly to control more than required, reducing the economy-wide cost of meeting a specific abatement target. Flexibility in implementation extends to the timing of upgrades as well. The ability to purchase emissions credits or to pay pollution taxes as an alternative to controlling emissions directly allows firms to coordinate their compliance investments more closely with the normal capital replacement cycle at the plant. This reduces premature capital equipment replacement and additional plant shutdown time. Governments also enjoy more flexibility with EIs: if the market does not sufficiently reduce emissions, governments can adjust the EIs by either increasing fees or decreasing permits. Such a process is generally much easier than trying to legislate changes to regulatory standards as would occur under a CAC approach.

- **Encouraged use of innovative abatement technologies**
  Because firms can control less pollution than the emissions target by paying extra taxes or fees, they face much lower financial risk from trying emerging technologies that may not work perfectly at first and miss the target control level. However, over a longer period of time, these unproven techniques often lead to more effective and less expensive control approaches. In addition, because excess reductions have financial value (reductions can be sold to others with emissions trading; tax bill declines with pollution taxes) firms have a continued incentive to innovate even if already in compliance.

- **Allocation of natural resources to parties who value them most**
  EIs that fairly auction access to publicly owned resources, be they oil, minerals, or grazing land, enable those who value them most to obtain them. If structured properly, these auction-based EIs encourage more sustainable use of flow resources (such as grasslands and water) and more careful use of stock resources (such as oil and coal), as well as raising revenues for the government.[7] In contrast, CACs often allocate

---

[6] OECD analysed numerous empirical studies on the efficiency gains associated with EIs, finding fairly strong evidence of beneficial impacts. (OECD, 1997, pp. 31). The gains associated with any specific EI, however, would be highly influenced by the specifics of the tool applied and the political context in which it was used.
[7] Although some of these approaches cannot be used for minerals found on private land, even on these private holdings there is social control over emissions and often on reclamation as well. Both of these areas offer fruitful options for EIs.

resources uniformly without much consideration of their relative value to different groups. One important caveat on the market-based transfers, however, is if they are structured *improperly* (such as when assets are transferred in rigged auctions or other corrupt methods at a fraction of true value; or when bonding for post-extraction remediation is not done), resource depletion can actually be accelerated.

- **Self-enforcement by aligning public and private interests**
  As noted above, EIs create groups of firms and individuals with vested interests in the proper use of resources and in emitting only as much pollution as allowed.[8] For example, firms that wish to sell excess pollution rights will watch to be sure that firms that need to buy rights do so. Mechanisms for granting or securing access to resources are also important. Groups that are given communal property rights in perpetuity have a greater incentive to ensure other people do not encroach on the land, and to manage assets for the long-term -- if only to protect the resale value of these rights. The effect is to create a more decentralized enforcement system for environmental policies, reducing the burden on the State.

- **Increased transparency**
  CACs often generate complex permits and reporting requirements, many of which are difficult for outside parties to obtain or to analyse. In contrast, the costs and rights associated with many EIs (pollution taxes, marketable permits) are more visible through trading levels, prices, ownership patterns, and fee receipts. As a result, evaluating investment trade-offs is easier to do, and lobbying for special privileges or exceptions becomes more difficult. Note that both types of policies still require effective monitoring, data generation, and enforcement functions, though the exact information collected may differ.

- **Cost-recovery of public provision of services**
  Publicly owned or delivered resources such as drinking water or oil are sold at market price, or at least at levels that recover the full cost of providing them. In addition to generating important revenues that can be used to finance continued provision of government services, the fees can also encourage increased conservation. Planning to mitigate impacts of new charges on impoverished citizens through subsidies is sometimes needed. However, in many cases existing systems do not reach the sections of the country with the poorest citizens who most need access to clean water or electricity due to lack of capital. Proper targeting and channelling of revenues to the poor segments of society is therefore essential. Proper cost recovery on the existing system also provide important financial stability to service debt needed for system expansion, or to finance such expansion directly.

2.3 Making sense out of EI options

EIs comprise a variety of policy approaches that "encourage behaviour through their impact on market signals rather than through explicit directives regarding pollution control levels or methods,"[9] or resource use. In practice, this encompasses many policy instruments including permits, quotas, licenses, concessions, user fees, use taxes, access fees, impact fees,

---

[8] For additional detail on this important incentive, see OECD, Domestic Tradable Permits for Environmental Management, 2001
[9] Robert Stavins, 2001, p. 1.

performance bonds, deposits, rights to sue, and financial assurance.[10] Product labelling/reporting are sometimes included as EIs as well.[11] Each of these instruments, in turn, has common variants. For example, any rights to access a resource or emit a pollutant can be marketable or non-marketable; they may be allocated by auction, or by past production level. The range of possibilities is large and potentially confusing.

Many existing studies group EIs by instrument type: permits, taxes, charges, deposit-refund systems, and the like. This report categories them instead by their *functional objective*, i.e., what they accomplish in the marketplace. The aim is to provide a more intuitive system by which policy makers can quickly narrow down their range of instruments once they have defined their problem.

EIs are basically structured to achieve some mixture of three main goals:
1) redressing problems with property rights that contribute to pollution or poor stewardship of resources;
2) establishing and enforcing prices for resources consumed and environmental damages associated with production;
3) subsidizing the transition to preferred behaviours.

In addition, many EIs have the added benefit that they generate revenues for the public sector. The text below provides a general overview of each of these goals and the way in which EIs can achieve them. This overview is supported by two additional references. First, the matrix in Exhibit 2.1 at the end of this chapter links the functional objectives to the market incentives, as well as identifies important factors for policy makers to consider when applying particular instrument types. Second, Annex A provides a detailed overview of the specific instruments within each EI grouping, along with the parameters commonly modified to refine the policy package. Some of the functional objectives of EIs are to:

- **Establish, clarify or improve property rights**
  Property rights entail a range of approaches (e.g., contracts, permits, rights to sue) that spell out who may do what with particular resources during a certain time period. Ensuring property rights are clear to all parties can add security and flexibility to the management of natural resources by removing pressures to "get what you can" while it is still there. Rights-related EIs allow owners to invest in the resources and to extract/harvest them at a more sustainable rate (though this does not always occur in practice). Importantly, property rights need not be individualized. For instance, communal property rights can also provide more secure tenure to impoverished indigenous population groups.

---

[10] See Annex A.

[11] Voluntary industry standards or labelling programmes are sometimes classified as EIs, because they modify demand through the provision of increased data on products to consumers in the marketplace. If voluntary programmes achieve a critical mass of participation and establish credible validation that stated commitments are being met, they can generate an effective impetus for environmental improvement. Often, however, these programmes lack any credible validation, establish symbolic targets with little environmental benefit, or engage only a small portion of the relevant industrial base. When this occurs, environmental benefits may be small, or even negative if the voluntary approach has diverted implementation of more rigorous controls, be they CACs or EIs. In addition, voluntary measures often face higher transaction costs to bring in partners, as well as foregoing the revenues that could otherwise have been generated through pollution fees or permits. See OECD, Environmentally Related Taxes in OECD Countries, 2001, p. 41.

- **Ensure that resource users pay a fair price for what they consume**

  Fees are the public sector's version of prices. Their function is the same: to recover the cost of providing goods and services from the groups that use them.[12] Often, many kinds of environmental fees and charges are lumped into a single category of instruments. Although all help clarify price signals and encourage efficient use of resources, different types of EIs aim to solve different problems. The elements are often additive; aggregate fees need to be high enough to achieve the appropriate cost recovery and environmental charges. The most efficient solutions in an economic sense occur when fees are set to recover both the direct costs of goods and services plus the environmental cost associated with producing and using a particular product. Although political realities often prevent this outcome, any of the steps below can improve the situation currently in effect.

  - *Recover the costs of government-provided goods and services.* Even before thinking about making a profit, private firms must cover their costs from the sale of their products in order to stay in business. This most basic of business principles is often ignored in the public sector, where users expect that drinking water, sewage treatment, or electricity should be heavily subsidized or free. User fees set to cover costs correct this problem. Though care is needed in rate design to ensure the poor have continued access to life sustaining services, there is little economic or environmental logic in subsidizing *all* customers.

  - *Ensure adequate return on sale of public assets.* When governments choose to sell assets, be they oil reserves in the ground or expansive government owned enterprises (e.g., electrical generating stations or oil refining facilities), it is critical that these sales earn appropriate returns on invested public capital, or on the sale of limited resources. When proceeds are earmarked at least in part to environmental protection measures, the environmental benefits can be further expanded. In the past these sales have all too often been used as financial payoffs to political supporters.

  - *Compensate public for/protect public from environmental damages caused by private production.* EIs such as pollution taxes help capture the societal costs (such as medical problems) that private firms cause by their emission of pollutants. They are effectively a charge for the use of the public resource of environmental quality. A number of litigation tools help recover costs for damages associated with past production. In addition, bonds and deposit/refund systems create financial assurance that taxpayers will not incur a debt if future producers do not properly clean up after their projects or products.

- **Subsidizing cleaner alternatives**

  There are many different EIs that can transfer resources from the public to the "preferred" private alternatives. If done properly, such efforts may be able to accelerate the development of these environmentally superior alternatives. However, great care is

---

[12] Setting appropriate fees is not always straightforward. To do so, public sector agencies must have acceptable accounting standards that give them an accurate view of their expenditures to provide particular services, at least on a gross level. Care is needed to ensure that the cost of capital (such as interest on public funds invested in infrastructure), liabilities, costs of public employees used on a project, and other similar costs are properly captured. In addition, governments should divide the recipients of their services into user classes to be sure that they are not taxing poor residential consumers unduly to pay for more expensive or difficult to provide services to industrial customers. This process is known as "rate design" and is widely used in the US to set electricity, water, and wastewater treatment tariffs.

needed to ensure that subsidies are appropriately targeted, only applied in the short-term, and do not end up making the problems worse instead of better.[13]

- **Generate revenue**

  Applying EIs (for example, pollution permits) can generate positive environmental outcomes whether or not the government is paid for the rights at the outset. However, where permits are actually sold to, or fees levied on, polluters new revenue streams to the government can be substantial. These can potentially help to enforce, improve, and expand environmental and resource protection programmes.

2.4 Summary

In most countries, CAC approaches dominate environmental policy-making. These approaches are often viewed as more "secure" in terms of addressing a particular environmental concern because they are proscriptive, although the causes of this dominance are probably more diverse. Blackman and Harrington (1998) note three factors supporting CAC dominance. First, market leaders may have stronger influence on the political process shaping CACs than with EIs. They point to the particular leverage in the developing world, where market leaders may be closely aligned with governments and the populace is accustomed to less efficient institutional systems. Damania (1999) points out that this process is also seen in the developed world. His work suggests that CACs are a more likely outcome unless politicians allied with environmentalists are in power or likely to come into power. CACs therefore give powerful factions more influence in shaping controls with little public opposition. Secondly, the monitoring requirements of CACs may be less sophisticated. For example, governments may simply need to confirm that a particular piece of pollution abatement equipment has been installed, rather than monitoring air emissions month after month to confirm compliance with permits. Thirdly, CAC is the status quo, and inertia prevents change.[14] CAC approaches may also dominate in part because they take a legal approach to behaviour modification, and as policy makers across the world tend to have legal backgrounds, such an approach is inherently logical to them. Additionally, the validity of EIs are sometimes called into question because they allow people to "pay to pollute".

Some of the claims supporting the use of CACs are open to challenge. For example, CACs require a sophisticated and corruption-free government to promulgate and enforce, a condition few countries have. In addition, because CACs set specific pollution limits, all emissions below that level are essentially free for the polluter. In contrast, most EIs price all units of pollution, and firms that go far below the allowable standards can resell incremental reductions to other parties. Paying for polluting emissions seems better than allowing firms to pollute for free as many CACs do. Futhermore, there is fairly convincing evidence that EIs have had minimal impacts on economic competitiveness and trade (Pearce, forthcoming). In fact, since EIs can generally achieve environmental targets at a lower cost than CACs, and generate technological innovation in the areas of pollution control and prevention they can generate positive effects on competitiveness and international trade.[15]

---

[13] For a detailed analysis on subsidies and their impacts, see recent UNEP publication *Energy Subsidies: Lessons Learned in Assessing their Impact and Designing Policy Reforms,* 2004.

[14] Blackman and Harrington, 1998, p. 6.

[15] Analysis by Esty and Porter (2001) found "no evidence that improving environmental quality compromises economic programme" but rather that "strong environmental performance appears to be positively correlated with competitiveness".

Because the potential benefits of EIs in terms of efficiency and long-term environmental improvement can be substantial, they merit careful consideration for new policy development or reforms of existing approaches. EIs can add flexibility, precision, and dynamism to policy packages and address a wide range of environmental problems. Rights to sue, creation of tradable permits, and granting of property rights to subsistence populations can all serve to provide a decentralized, non-governmental enforcement mechanism to ensure environmental responsibilities are upheld, a great help in countries with severely limited enforcement budgets. Pollution taxes and marketable permits can help reduce water, air and land pollution and provide effective ways for pollution reduction activities to be concentrated in firms with the lowest costs of abatement. By making compliance less expensive, pollution reduction can be less of a burden to both governments and the private sector, less of a competitive factor in trade, and of great benefit to both developed and developing nations. Lower costs also make it possible for countries to achieve a higher level of environmental protection than would otherwise be possible. The process of narrowing policy options to fit specific problems is addressed in the next chapter.

Exhibit 2.1

Impact of EIs on incentives of firms and individuals

Functional impact of EIs	Examples	Factors in application
1. Establish, clarify, or improve property rights: creating markets for unpriced resources and environmental services to provide incentives for sustainable management and use; establish clear rules for resource access to control overuse.		
-Invest for the long term. Clear property rights enable owners to benefit from longer-term investment and management of a resource. **-Curb tragedy of the commons.** In many cases, property rights approaches eliminate the "tragedy of the commons" problem, in which unlimited access destroys the common resource base. **-Incentive to control as much as possible.** In the case of pollution permits, the rights enable people to profit from reducing pollution more than required under current laws. **-Manage for future owners.** So long as rights can be sold, owners have an incentive to continue to manage the property carefully in order to attain a high resale value. This also provides some incentive to avoid accidents and post-closure contamination. **-Independent enforcement.** Ability to enforce rights through litigation can ensure make rights regimes more effective without needing central government intervention.	-Granting formal harvest rights to indigenous populations or allowing transfer of existing rights. -Establishing and requiring tradable permits or licenses for parameters of concern (e.g., plant emissions, fishing access). -Allowing farmers to sell existing water rights to urban areas. -Establishing or enforcing rights to sue parties (including the government) for violation of existing property rights.	-Granting property rights is meaningless unless there is a fair court system to enforce them. -Where courts are strong, granting of authority/right to sue to third parties can overcome weak administrative ministries. -Monitoring of many rights regimes (e.g., fisheries, emissions) can be complicated and substantial. -How initial rights are to be distributed is often controversial, and can generate windfalls to existing producers that may be viewed as inequitable or that put small business at a competitive disadvantage. -Ensuring that rights are transferable is important in establishing a strong incentive for long-term management. A secondary market in rights ensures regular repricing of rights and continued efforts to reduce permits needed if prices are high.

Functional impact of EIs	Examples	Factors in application
2A. Recover direct costs of environmental services or oversight provided by public agencies from the beneficiaries: policies ensure that users see realistic costs for the publicly-provided services they are using.		
-Self-sustaining revenues. Charging for services earns important revenues enabling the continued provision of critical municipal services without having to fully privatize the functions. **-Incentive to conserve.** These charges also send more accurate price signals to consumers that help conserve resources such as energy and water, and allow existing infrastructure capacity to last longer as demand falls. **-Costs borne by sub-groups responsible.** Ensuring that higher-cost user groups (high peak demands; high requirements for government oversight; more complex discharges for treatment plant; higher distribution costs; etc.) pay more refines price signals further.	-Recover full costs of municipal energy, water, sewerage, solid waste services from customers. This must include real cost of financing construction. -Charge higher rates to higher cost customers. -Narrow consumption subsidies to target only the poorest users of the product or service. -Sell government owned enterprises to the private sector to correct pricing problems. Ensure continued service to poor via direct subsidies or regulatory oversight.	-Many countries face political barriers to implementing and enforcing equitable user charges. -Privatization can be one solution to overcome this problem, but is not possible without rule of law. In addition, states must be careful to avoid privately-owned monopoly providers by ensuring there are multiple vendors. -Recovery of aggregate costs will not be efficient if certain user groups receive cross-subsidies from others in the rate structure. -Enterprises must be able to retain receipts for reinvestment (rather than remitting to the Treasury) if the EIs are to help ensure the enterprise's continued existence.
2B. Receive just compensation for sale of publicly owned assets to private sector entities: policies ensure taxpayers are fairly treated in purchases, and that purchasing entities make resource development/consumption decisions based on realistic prices.		
-Tap revenues for general society. EIs that create markets and transparency for the sale of publicly owned assets ensure that the returns from these sales go to the general population rather than to political or military elites. **-Reduce opportunities for corruption.** Transparent procedures can also help reduce or eliminate the ability for corruption to flourish. **-Rational development path.** Because political and military power for individuals is often short-lived, individuals may rush natural resource extraction to maximize diversions to personal wealth. Transparent markets encourage a more rational development path.	-Elimination of all resource giveaways above a certain size. Registration and tracking for small subsistence extraction. -Natural resource auctions open to all bidders, including international firms or non users such as environmental groups who wish to remove resource from production. -Establish three part fee structure: bounties to cover initial rights; rental to cover holding cost of resource access; and royalties to share returns on extracted resources. -Open bidding on any infrastructure privatization efforts.	-In countries with high corruption, much of the returns on both public resource deposits and cash flows from nationalized industries are diverted to finance political interests. As such, reforms can be difficult. -However, pressure from outside funders or investors can play a positive role in ensuring some of this change occurs. -Some portion of receipts should support continued environmental management.

Functional impact of EIs	Examples	Factors in application
2C. Establish financial charges and accountability for environmental harm: policies internalize the cost of environmental damages and the risk of potential damages.		
-Polluter pays more than under CAC. In many CAC systems, at least a portion of the pollution is granted to corporations for free (the amount from zero up to the statutory limit). Charges and financial accountability force more of the social and environmental costs of polluting activities to be reflected in the price of the associated products, increasing the incentive to develop cleaner products. **-Incentive to leave site in good condition.** Performance bonds and other mechanisms establish financial responsibility for clean-up prior to the beginning of a project, greatly reducing the public sector risk from negligence. **-Responsible for natural resource damage/non-compliance.** Legal controls can create a "market" in compliance enforcement, empowering third parties to bring suit for environmental non-compliance.	<u>Current activity</u> -Pollution taxes/permits <u>Past activity</u> -Civil and criminal penalties for natural resource damages <u>Future activity</u> -Required liability or environmental insurance -Performance bonds for proper site remediation/closure -Deposit/refund systems for proper product returns.	-Pollution taxes are often difficult to set at appropriate levels, and require an effective bureaucracy to monitor. -Care is needed to avoid "hot spots" where the local environment and/or populace is subject to excessively high emissions as a result of the trading or charge schemes. -Financial assurance and deposit/refund systems require enforcement of rules in order to work. This may not be possible in high-corruption environments. -Care is needed to identify and monitor the credit quality of providers of financial assurance. -Governments may need to stipulate the required terms of coverage in order for financial assurance mechanisms to be effective. -Third-party legal suits can be abused.

Functional impact of EIs	Examples	Factors in application
3. Subsidize transition to, or investment in, more sustainable alternatives: policies promote mechanisms that can accelerate the development and adoption of cleaner technologies using both direct funding and government programmes.		
-**Cleaner products faster.** Can accelerate the development and/or market adoption of improved products or production methods. -**Reduced burden of transition.** Can reduce transition costs for private parties to invest in new production methods. -**Poverty amelioration.** Where the poor will be adversely affected by the change, subsidies can help cushion the pain from the shift. -**Pay private stewards of important global resources.** Can compensate parties or countries for foregoing private gain in order to steward resources with high social values (e.g., biodiversity).	-Fiscal subsidies including grants, loans, loan guarantees, indemnification, or tax breaks. -Forgiveness of environmental fees, taxes, royalties, penalties in return for investments in environmental improvement. -Differential tax rates depending on environmental impact of the product.	-Everybody wants subsidies and can make some claim to justify why they need it. Care is needed to provide a much narrowed conceptualization of the market segments requiring public subsidy. -Where subsidies are provided, they must be transparent and trackable. They should also phase out automatically after a pre-specified period of time. -Where transitional subsidies are to be paid as a political price for accepting policy changes, these must be evaluated carefully to curb excesses and confirm there are no alternatives.

Source: Earth Track, Inc, commissioned by UNEP, 2004.

3. Policy Design and Implementation

One of the most difficult challenges facing policy makers is choosing an effective policy package that will both address the environmental problem they are facing and fit in with the existing institutional capabilities and environmental policies. Country analysts have noted that often there is no formal process of evaluation at all prior to recommending a particular policy approach. The goal of this chapter is to provide a framework for conducting policy design, implementation and evaluation.

There is always a balance to be struck between analysing a problem and moving forward with a solution. Further research can refine the approach, but requires extra time during which environmental damage continues, and more money that many governments do not have. Making sense out of varied and disparate information can be challenging, but the ability to maximize what can be learned from existing data is extremely valuable in achieving sound policies with minimal lead times. Using the approaches presented in this chapter, policy makers should be able to make better use of information they already have, identify key areas where there are informational gaps, and quickly focus their work on a narrow set of promising policies.

Policy choice and implementation encompasses four main phases. Phase 1 involves assembling existing information in a structured way. Creating this structure is a critical step, as it drives the process of assessing the solutions that may work from those that may not, as well as the identification of key data gaps. Phase 2 takes the general information provided by Phase 1 and uses it to develop initial policy proposals. Phase 3 brings in stakeholders for feedback on these initial options, and collects important information on how to refine them to increase their likelihood of success or to gauge any major resistance. This input is then fed back into the information bank developed in Phase 1.

Phase 4 is the process of implementation. This involves establishing from the outset a strict timeline for implementing the chosen policy package. Parallel work to ensure effective monitoring and enforcement needs also to occur. Similarly, additional work on any flanking measures needed to assess impacts of the change on poverty or international competitiveness may also be required. The four phases are described in detail below.

3.1   Phase 1: Assembling existing information in a structured way

Country-level policy makers often have better information about the issues they are facing than they think at first; the challenge is putting it together in a meaningful way. Careful consideration regarding problem definition and the interests of various stakeholder groups can prove valuable. Some key questions to ask are presented below, followed by a sample template to organize the data in a way that makes the choices, information gaps, and trade-offs clear to see.

- **What is the goal?** Goal definition should include a primary goal, e.g. to curb over-fishing and ensure future catches are sustainable, and any secondary goals that may be relevant. Secondary goals might include protecting subsistence fishermen or coastal fishing communities. While primary goals are generally related to human health and the environment, secondary goals often relate to poverty reduction, job protection/creation, or preserving culture or community. In some circumstances, secondary goals can be cleanly blended into policy. Most times, however, trade-offs are needed.

- **What are the baseline conditions?** The appropriate policy response hinges on a clear and realistic understanding of the baseline conditions. While it is possible to improve institutional capacity to address existing weaknesses, doing so is a difficult and a time consuming process, diverting resources from the primary environmental goals. Though every country wants to portray an image of clean and efficient governance, few nations can truly boast such systems. The level of competence and corruption for any area/institution that will be used to develop, promulgate, monitor, or enforce the policy in question needs to be realistically assessed. A number of international metrics (presented in Annex B) are also being developed, and can support internal judgments in a more politically sensitive way.

  - *Institutional baselines.* Many EIs rely on functioning tax, legal, or fiscal systems. Despite being more efficient in theory, if the institutional capabilities needed to promulgate and enforce the EIs in a fair and unbiased manner are lacking, the performance of the EIs will suffer. One caveat is that CACs also rely on many of these same factors, and policy comparisons should take common weaknesses into account when evaluating options.

  - *Mandate and level of power.* Many environmental protection packages come from the environment ministries, which generally have far less political power than finance or trade ministries. Powerful interests also reside in the heads of the executive and legislative branches, all of whom may try to use the power of government to appease or compensate particular constituencies at the expense of environmental quality. Policy makers need to assess their relative power accurately and plan how to address their weaknesses. For example, approaches that generate revenues as well as solve environmental problems can bring in allies in the fiscal ministries that would not otherwise come forward.

  - *Factional analysis.* Policy changes involve far more than government bodies. Assessing the major players with an interest in the status quo, and in the projected change, is important. This baseline assessment should also evaluate which groups are most powerful, and what their primary goal is likely to be. In many cases, their primary goal will be linked to protection of their jobs and/or access to valuable resources. Environmental quality may be a distant second. Allocation of rights in the baseline is also quite important: groups with existing rights (whether actual or implied) will often have more power/interest in fighting changes to existing policies. The factional analysis should also assess what options exist for buffering any transitional dislocations (especially affecting the poor) that may occur from the policy reform. Initial thinking about the major interest groups should be done during Phase 1 in order to identify obvious roadblocks that could affect the choice of reasonable policy options. Refinements will be incorporated during Phase 3 when stakeholder outreach begins.

- **What is the long-term viability of the package?** Countries may receive external funding to conduct policy research or to implement EI-based approaches. However, this money does not last forever. A long-term plan for implementing and overseeing the policy should be considered at the outset. Because different policy options can place very different long-term monitoring and enforcement responsibilities on the government, advance attention can ensure a more robust policy solution in the long term, rather than one for which adequate funding will be a perpetual problem.

The key sections of the template presented in Exhibit 3.1 include the problem definition and a detailed evaluation of baseline conditions. Initial completion of the template should be based on existing knowledge or impressions, enabling policy makers to identify information gaps. The template then becomes a guideline to the process of policy development, incorporating the views of stakeholders, and then implementing the policy package.

Exhibit 3.1

Template for assessing important factors affecting instrument choice

Issue	Clarifying questions	Implications on policy choice and application of EIs
A. Assessing the problem		
What is the damaged resource?	-Are there human health considerations? -Are pollutant emissions of concern? -Does it cause ecosystem degradation or destruction? -Is there a lack of control over resource use/depletion path?	-Exposure to particular emissions of concern would require more detailed assessment of the sources of emissions to assess appropriate control strategy. -Ecosystem degradation can often be addressed through property-rights approaches that generate an economic interest in long-term resource management. -Gaining control of development path may require a mix of increased transparency, adequate cost recovery on government provided goods and services, and third party rights to sue.
What is the anticipated severity of damage?	-Are dangers acute and severe, or less severe but persistent? -Are the damages irreversible?	-The more acute the potential damage, the more important a rapid response is needed. This would argue for mandated controls quickly. Even if the initial controls cause some peripheral economic losses, the avoidance of the acute risks (e.g., ecosystem collapse, large and widespread human health damage) makes the choice a prudent one.
What does the government hope to accomplish?	-Do emissions need to be reduced or stopped entirely? -Are resource pressures to be reduced quickly or slowly? -What social, political, or economic constraints is the government likely to face in meeting its goals?	-EIs are most appropriate for longer-term, gradual controls for emissions. However, property rights regimes can place quite rapid constraints on the rate of exploitation. -Where non-environmental constraints are substantial, early analysis and stakeholder meetings should provide sufficient attention to this area.
Pollutant characteristics (where control target is pollutant-based)	-Pollutant name, toxicity, dispersion profile (e.g., to air, land, water).- Separable from other waste streams (treatment options)? -Is it measurable? Is it possible to monitor? -Are there Potential reuse markets?	-Highly toxic agents require tighter controls. EIs such as rebates can be used if target wastes are discrete and separable agents. If part of general emissions, CAC approaches such as bans or severe restrictions warranted.

Issue	Clarifying questions	Implications on policy choice and application of EIs
	-Are product markets price sensitive?	-Reuse markets increase the economic viability of recovering and reusing the constituents of concern, and suggest advance deposits or take-back programs could be effective. -More price sensitive products (i.e., commodities) will often be unable to pass increased emissions control costs through to customers by raising prices. Political resistance to any controls likely to be higher in these types of product markets.
Resources at risk (where control target is resource area)	-What is (are) the resource(s) being exploited? -What peripheral natural assets are threatened? -Is exploitation threatening a widespread collapse of the ecosystem? Is the potential damage irreversible? -Is resource of primary value to the local community or to a more global set of beneficiaries (e.g., biodiversity)? -Are resource owners (including the taxpayer) adequately compensated for the current/planned resource exploitation?	-Over-exploitation can often be addressed through the granting/clarification of property rights. Where wide-spread or irreversible collapse is imminent, extreme action may be needed to curb exploitation immediately (e.g., fishing bans). During interim period, more flexible licensing/permit approaches can be developed. -Ecosystem-wide view is generally needed to ensure that the entire basket of resources are appropriately addressed by the policy. -Where resources under threat benefit regional, national, or international interests much more than local extractors, financial payments from the beneficiaries to protect the resources are often warranted. -Ensuring appropriate pricing of access can have the double benefit of reducing development pressure and raising some revenues to support ongoing management.

B. Factional analysis: Who are the stakeholders, what are their interests?

1. Understanding the source of the environmental threat

Issue	Clarifying questions	Implications on policy choice and application of EIs
Profile of emissions source (industry/household/ government/mobile source)	-Is emissions source comprised of a small number of large firms or is it a cottage industry?	environmental controls. EIs such as marketable permits are one way around this, so long as the government can set a realistic cap on

Issue	Clarifying questions	Implications on policy choice and application of EIs
	-Do international firms comprise a large percentage of domestic production? -What are the firm's incentives for being in the host country? -How large is the market share of government owned entities? -What is the ownership structure of mobile source threats (e.g., individual cars vs. fleet-owned trucks)?	allowable permits. -For specialized pollutants with only a handful of sources, direct regulation using a CAC approach may be most beneficial. -Fragmented and/or impoverished sources generally require more outreach and transitional strategies. -International firms are the most sensitive to informational approaches that can harm their brand image globally. However, firm location may be due to lax environmental or fiscal oversight. -Government owned entities are often not subject to strict financial performance. Difficult to modify behaviour using EIs, though political resistance to CACs also likely to be high.
Cause of overuse of existing resource base	-Is overuse the result of activities by large corporations, or by large numbers of subsistence extractors? -Does the public receive market-value for resources extracted/sold? -Are extractive firms financially liable for damages they cause to natural resources in the course of their activities? -Is domestic industry under pressure from unfair competition (subsidized, unregulated) from abroad?	-Exploitation by subsistence extractors can be addressed through the granting of property rights (often communal), subject to proper land management. -For all extractors, ensuring appropriate fees for activities helps encourage appropriate exploitation rates. In countries where these funds are diverted as kickbacks, policies to improve financial transparency (e.g., independent auditors) can help. -Financial assurance mechanisms, such as performance bonds, provide market-based leverage to ensure proper site management and cleanup. -Litigation tools, such as citizen suits, can take the profit out of poor environmental management, though there is some potential risk of too much litigation resulting.
2. Government institutions		
Which government institutions have an interest in the exploitation	-Environmental ministries are often in charge of overseeing whatever control method is chosen.	-Environmental ministries may have a limited mandate over the definition of acceptable control methods and the deployment

Issue	Clarifying questions	Implications on policy choice and application of EIs
or regulation of the issue of concern?	-Are international firms from major powers part of the problem? -Are products associated with the resource damage exported internationally for hard currency? -If there will be revenues raised (through the sale of permits, implementation of pollution taxes, or charges for government-provided goods and services), who will get them?	of collected revenues. -Where international firms are involved in market, environmental controls may be undermined by foreign-government lobbying efforts. Ample use of publicity in these circumstances can provide leverage. -Where domestic export earnings may be affected, expect intervention from trade and finance ministries. Pollution permits or taxes, by providing increased flexibility and lower costs, can be advantageous here.
Linkage to public infrastructure	Does sector rely on public infrastructure (water, wastewater treatment, electricity, roads)? Which ones, and in what way?	Can provide important information on possible leverage points for user charges, permit modifications, etc.
3. Employees	-Does the affected sector employ large numbers of subsistence workers? Does it produce products on which the poor rely? -Are the affected industries unionized? -Does the proposed change open up significant new employment opportunities?	-Careful planning on transition strategies is needed if changes to resource access threatens large numbers of jobs. Where population pressure is not too large, property rights regimes can concurrently encourage improved natural resource extraction and improve employment prospects. -Unionized workforces may resist change by either CAC or EIs. To the extent that EIs allow less expensive compliance by firms, it may be preferable to unions, as job losses may be lower. -Government owned enterprises in many countries are stagnant and corrupt. Privatization can eliminate kick-back schemes and spur new innovation and employment opportunities. Expect strong political resistance, and ensure privatization process is transparent and competitive to avoid the privatization itself transferring massive wealth through corruption.

Issue	Clarifying questions	Implications on policy choice and application of EIs
C. Overview of public sector institutions: Structure and strength		Applies to local, regional, or national institutions, depending on problem being addressed.
1. General. Overview of Government Employees and Ministerial Coordination	-Professional civil service? Widespread bribe taking? -At what level of government (national, provincial, local) does the operational power reside? -Are institutions fragmented or capable of working together?	-Poorly-trained, corrupt, or fragmented civil service imply that greater reliance on decentralized oversight would be necessary. -Conflicts between the government level issuing a policy and the one with power increases the likelihood of being over-ruled. -International metrics, such as by Transparency International, can highlight these issues. Should be supported by private assessments as well.
2. Legal institutions		
Legal: Rule of Law	-Does the legal system enforce laws on the books generally? -Do citizens have legal recourse for damages they incur at the hands of private or municipal corporations?	Without the rule of law generally applied, the chance of succeeding with any type of environmental instrument (EI or CAC) is likely to be small.
Legal: Scope of Authority	-What legal platform will support EI programs? Are there any known barriers? -Is the polluter pays principle or other methods that hold polluters responsible for environmental harm within the existing legal system?	Understanding the scope of legal authority is important in order to make realistic decisions about what types of policy actions will be possible without difficult-to-obtain changes in legal mandates or in the national constitution.
Legal: Enforcement of Property Rights	-Does the legal system specifically enforce property rights?	Without property rights, there can be no use of marketable permits, and firms/other entities will have little incentive to invest large sums in pollution-control plant and equipment.
Legal: Right to sue violators	-Can third parties (e.g., individuals, environmental groups, other firms) sue companies that are violating environmental laws already on the books? -Can suits be brought for general damages to natural resources?	Litigation can leverage the oversight power of governments by allowing other parties to take action as well. It can serve as a useful check and balance for other policies to make them more effective, be they CAC or EI.

Issue	Clarifying questions	Implications on policy choice and application of EIs
3. Fiscal/economic institutions		
Fiscal: Functioning tax and financial reporting/audit system	-Are general taxes levied by the central authority and paid by the private sector? -Is there general confidence in the financial representations of private and municipal corporations? -Are the incentives provided by the current fiscal regime supportive or antagonistic to the new EI instrument?	-If nobody pays regular taxes, there is little chance they will pay environmental taxes. -Widespread perverse incentives will undermine the effectiveness of many EI (or CAC) approaches. -If the information presented by firms is inaccurate and subject to no penalties, only very centralized environmental policies would work (e.g., product fees, technology mandates).
Fiscal: Functioning insurance markets	-Can insurance be purchased at reasonable rates for a wide range of common business risks? -Is there any environmental risk coverage at all?	Functioning insurance markets can help reduce the need for direct-government oversight. Performance bonds, environmental liability policies, etc., can provide decentralized control methods.
Economic: Macroeconomic conditions of concern	-Is there hyperinflation? -Are poverty levels high? -Is there high unemployment? -Do resource sales provide critical foreign exchange earnings? -Is there a high national debt level?	-Any of these factors tend to diminish the relative importance of environmental issues. Because poverty and unemployment may also result from widespread corruption and poor governance, there may be ways to incorporate environmental EIs in a broad-scale reform package. -Natural resource sales are often a large source of foreign exchange, and production facilities are often owned by the government. This makes environmental controls of any kind very difficult to institute.
4. Environmental	-Centralized authority with direct power and direct voice to head of government? -Are there existing laws on the books? Are these adequately enforced? Are there existing laws on ambient environmental conditions, resource consumption, environmental permits, and enterprise emissions generally available to the public? -Is there a functioning monitoring and reporting system for measurement of baseline environmental data?	-Fragmentation of oversight amongst multiple agencies (e.g., environmental impact of agriculture, forestry, or mining managed elsewhere) greatly weakens the power to bring about environmental change. -Direct voice with the head of state also important to increase leverage to initiate sometimes difficult changes. -Where there are extensive existing environmental laws that are not enforced, these same problems with authority are likely to plague any new efforts (whether EI or CAC). -Lack of information will impair the ability to implement or oversee a wide range of environmental policies, and will prevent many third-party enforcement approaches.

Source: Earth Track, Inc, commissioned by UNEP, 2004.

3.2   Phase 2: Moving from the template to draft policy options

The purpose of assembling information in Phase 1 is to help policy makers to develop a short-list of policy options. This list includes options that have the most reasonable chance of success given the existing baseline conditions and resources at risk. The initial drafts of the template should be able to identify plausible options, a great improvement over unsubstantiated guess work that many country analysts admit too often drive policy solutions now. Further refinement of policy options and packages will use feedback from Phase 3. This stage should also be more targeted and efficient with a structured approach.

Moving to make concrete policy choices is not always easy. Because every situation is different, it is difficult to offer specific guidance on how to do this. However, some general guidelines can help policy makers to choose the most appropriate options for further consideration.[16] These include specifically the recognition of policy trade-offs and realistic assessments of policy limitations.

Recognizing policy trade-offs

All policy packages involve trade-offs. For example, losses in the efficiency of an instrument must be balanced against the ease and timeliness of implementation given social and political realities. Similarly, in order to make packages acceptable to key parties, subsidies are sometimes included, even if not all are targeted to help the most vulnerable population segments during the transitional phase. Describing these trade-offs for a particular situation is useful to ensure full consideration of the implications of a decision and the implicit compromises they contain. Similarly, evaluating alternative solutions is important. For example, rather than providing subsidies to affected sectors, a gradual phase-in of policies can also reduce the transition costs without public expenditure. The following should be assessed for the different policy options:

- **Environmental effectiveness**

  Although compromises may be necessary, how well the proposal achieves its primary environmental objective should remain at the core when determining which options are acceptable. Periodic re-evaluation is needed, as strong lobbying efforts can sometimes quietly supplant secondary or tertiary objectives for the core environmental one, eroding the effectiveness of the policy over time.

- **Policy windows**

  As noted in Chapter 2, laws and regulations take a long time to implement, and getting rid of them entirely is not likely to happen. Thus, policy makers should look for ways to apply EIs within the broader existing rules. Panayotou identifies three main windows of opportunity: improving the efficiency and flexibility of existing regulations; improving cost recovery (with associated revenues earmarked for the environmental purposes they were raised from); and addressing problems not covered by existing regulations.[17] While these solutions may be less effective than if policy responses could be designed from scratch, the windows approach reflects political realities and provides a foothold for more effective environmental protection. In many cases, demonstrating success for EIs at the margin can generate the political will to expand their role over time.

---

[16] Many of these come from Panayotou, 1998, pp. 102-109.
[17] Ibid. p. 3.

- **Ease of introduction**

  Even without constraints posed by existing environmental legislation, environmental controls are often broadly opposed by various interest groups. Extensive conflict can greatly water down initiatives and long gestation periods can allow environmental damage to occur unchecked in the interim. In many cases, the opposition interests actually grow more organized and powerful during the delays, preventing the ability to make meaningful change. Policies that achieve slightly less, but are acted upon much more quickly, may therefore be beneficial. In addition, EIs have the advantage in that they can be incrementally made more stringent (e.g., in the case of tradable permits, by removing some of the existing permits) over time. One strategy is to have them less stringent initially to reduce opposition, but becoming more restrictive automatically over a 3-5 year period. The longer phase-in can also help keep implementation costs lower. Nearly every case study evaluated here had gestation periods far longer than that, generally due to attempts to resolve political disagreements. Thus, even a 5-year delay may be shorter than the time needed to move through the political process if it is a contentious one.[18]

- **Acceptability by key parties**

  Although the exact stakeholders will differ by country and problem area, they will generally involve industry and economic interest groups, government, workers, social and environmental welfare organizations, and general citizens. These groups will need to have some general acceptance of the policy path, though full consensus should not be the goal. Policy makers need to be cognizant of which groups have the most power and work around these constraints to achieve the policy objectives. Reliable data on the sources of environmental damage is extremely helpful in this regard. Attention should also be paid to highly impacted groups or individuals: low skilled workers may be thrown from work as environmental controls take effect; population centres near old plants may see exposures rise as inefficient plants in the cluster purchase emissions credits. Policy proposals should include appropriate flanking measures to ameliorate these impacts, for example transitional support for displaced individuals or poor segments of society. Solutions should adhere to the PPP as closely as possible, resisting the inevitable efforts by industry groups to have their entire transition costs shifted to the taxpayer. Acceptability can be enhanced if policies have an easy-to-understand technical basis; the oversight agency demonstrates adequate capabilities to perform the monitoring and evaluation tasks for which it is responsible; and credible financial penalties and sanctions are introduced.

Make realistic assessments of policy limitations

Chosen policies should incorporate realistic assessments of the limitations both of the policy instruments themselves and the institutions that will be overseeing them.[19] These include:

- **Match policy plans to institutional capabilities**

  Expectations must match the supporting capabilities of baseline institutions. Sometimes this may mean a less effective policy on a theoretical basis is actually the most appropriate one given institutional capabilities. If limitations are not recognized, the likelihood that the new instruments will fail is much higher, leaving the underlying

---

[18] One caveat: the stronger interest groups will often try to slow or eliminate the increased stringency before it takes effect. Initial policies need to anticipate this pressure and deal with it from the outset.

[19] The questions posed in Exhibit 3.1 can help make these assessments.

environmental problem unsolved. While institutional growth is possible, assuming extensive changes to the structure or performance of these institutions in the solutions promoted may be unrealistic. Simpler solutions are best where they will do the job. If the problem is local, local solutions may be best as well. If the problem involves a handful of industries with similar production processes, establishing a national trading system probably does not make sense as costs of control will be similar across plants. Analysing cash flows associated with the policy can be helpful in making realistic assessments of existing institutional leverage. If revenues are to be collected, how are fees to be set? Who will collect the money, and do they have appropriate experience? Will the revenues be linked to solving the environmental problem, or simply diverted to the Treasury? Where the promulgating or implementing institutions control neither the budget nor the revenues on any instruments implemented, overcoming powerful opponents will be quite difficult. Solutions that generate new revenues, or that establish new markets (such as permits) where polluters must compete against each other rather than requiring extensive ministry oversight can in this case be helpful.

- **Predictability**

  Policy proposals should have clear rules for current applications. The goal is to establish a predictable and transparent path of controls for market participants and citizens alike. This facilitates long-term planning and investment, increasing the efficiency of the rules. Because knowledge about the environmental and health risks of particular activities will continue to grow, it is important that proposals can be modified to incorporate this new information. However, the process for doing so should be established up-front.

- **Economic instruments do not fit all situations**

  While the templates focus on applications of EIs, understanding when they are not appropriate (or when they require regulatory safeguards as flanking measures) is equally important. The following points can help narrow the list of policy options:

  - *Emergency conditions.* When problems have severe implications, emergency conditions arise, and behaviour needs to stop immediately, directive bans may be more appropriate. Where some activity, albeit a much lower level, would be acceptable, property rights or licensing approaches could work.

  - *Excessive monitoring costs.* Where monitoring costs are too high to achieve a specific environmental outcome, as when there are a large number of very small transactions (e.g., emissions trades), CACs may be a better fit. Similarly, where there are a very small number of homogenous parties, emissions trading would not have an effective market and few efficiency gains would be achieved through trading. Monitoring and oversight costs would exceed the benefit of EIs.

  - *Fragmented oversight authority.* Where authority to set and enforce regulations is highly fragmented across institutions, oversight of market-based instruments might become quite difficult. CACs tailored to the existing oversight authorities might be more efficient, though it is likely that such a policy approach would not be well integrated.

  - *Social stigma.* Societal factors can also make market-based approaches more difficult. For example, communal societies may not adapt well to individual members of the society holding particular rights or paying particular fees. In other societies, the activities that would be affected by the EIs may have a close link to social status, generating strong resistance to change. An example is the loss of cattle (and with it prestige) if market-based grazing rights are used. However, in these circumstances, EIs might work when applied at the community level since the communal decision making process can maintain the existing social hierarchy as access rights are granted.

- *Strong opposition.* Where political power and interest group factions remain strong, policy makers need to judge the most prudent course. Political power can be used when establishing EIs to generate loopholes, exemptions or windfalls, in exactly the same way as this power is applied in CACs. Privatization can be used as a front for corrupt sales to transfer state-owned assets to private parties with no gain to the public.

- *High level of dislocation.* Where large numbers of people will be displaced or unemployed as a result of EIs, caution is required. Regulatory exemptions, transitional payments, or some other flanking measure is needed to ameliorate potential hardships, especially for the poor.

- *No ability to make transitional payments to affected sectors.* From an economic perspective, it is more efficient to remove broad-based subsidies and replace them with direct payments to the poor. The link between the subsidy and resource use is removed, and public resources are targeted to the sub-sector in most need rather than to society as a whole. Examples include transitional subsidies to water, energy, foodstuffs for the poor segment of society. However, in corrupt societies, the transfer payments to the poor are unlikely to actually occur. Thus, monitoring and enforcement are essential to avoid broad based subsidies remain to avoid widespread hardship or social unrest.

3.3   Phase 3: Engaging stakeholders and refining policy choice

Assessment of the key interested parties occurs as a part of Phase 1, referred to as "factional analysis". That work is a starting point for the more complicated and delicate efforts to engage these groups in a process of evaluating and refining the initial list of policy choices. This feedback is then used to refine the informational templates and policy choices iteratively, resulting in a more appropriate set of instruments.

The stakeholder process requires consideration and control over two central issues: who to involve and how to structure their input. The process of organizing stakeholder involvement, however, will largely vary with the country in question and its cultural traditions and political climate.

Who to involve

Stakeholders should represent all of the core viewpoints on the issues to be addressed. This does not mean that every stakeholder must be involved (a complicated and expensive process), but only that the main viewpoints should be assembled through a variety of contact methods. Though there are many stakeholder groups (citizens, businesses, resource users, etc.), most issues will have three main stakeholder interests: those responsible for the problem; those affected by the problem; or those affected by one of the proposed solutions.

Within each of these categories, there may be stakeholders who are well organized and economically powerful as well as those who are not. The more organized parties will tend to have direct and concentrated interests in either keeping things as they are (e.g., companies who do not want to reduce their emissions) or from modifying regulation in a specific manner (e.g., companies making pollution control equipment who would benefit from more stringent regulations). A handful of very large firms will tend to be more powerful in opposition to change than a large number of small businesses. If the firms are controlled by people with ties to the government, the potential for them to bias the policy direction will be even larger. The challenge with the more powerful groups is in ensuring they are not able to derail the policy entirely through influencing the structure of the rules or instruments or by perpetual delaying tactics.

The voices most often missing entirely from the discussion are the uneducated, the unorganized, and the economically poor. These groups have neither the financial resources nor the skills to carefully evaluate planned government actions. Often they are fragmented and powerless, unable to play a role in the evolution of the policy package without explicit government effort. Yet, these are generally the very same groups most affected by the lack of environmental controls or by the planned policy changes. Financing participation in meetings, providing public access internet facilities or visiting geographic areas where the poor are concentrated to keep these parties abreast or involve them in decisions and emerging issues, or other methods that ensure information flows to and from this group can be useful. As many of the poor are concentrated within particular geographic areas, simply walking around and talking to people can be a valuable, low-cost way to gather and share information.

Making stakeholder input useful

Stakeholder input serves two main functions: it provides an important factual input into policy design and implementation; and it provides a venue for affected parties to speak about what are often contentious and even quite emotional issues. Both of these objectives can be achieved more effectively with some advance preparation, along the following guidelines:

- **Solicit input early.** Beginning discussions with stakeholders early in the process is helpful, even if these contacts are informal. This sends a very important signal that the government officials will make decisions in an informed and unbiased manner.

- **Use a variety of outreach methods.** Stakeholder engagements can be done through formal meetings, and such meetings can play an important role in allowing affected parties to air their concerns publicly. However, more frequent, less formal contacts and briefings may be more effective as an information gathering tool, keeping the process moving forward and facilitating iterative policy refinements. Less formal contacts also allow people to provide information more anonymously, which can encourage more forthright sharing of views.

- **Be clear with stakeholders about how information will be used.** As noted earlier, the stakeholder outreach should be viewed as an informational tool to support an informed decision, not a way to necessarily reach a policy consensus. Consensus building can easily become a tactic for affected parties to delay any action or activity, and making it clear that the governing agency is not focused on this aspect per se can help avoid unnecessary bottlenecks.

- **Set up a structured process and stick to it.** This includes transparency and a pre-set formal timeline for sharing information and comments.

Transparency. The overall policy assessment process must be done transparently. This helps stakeholders know that they will be heard fairly, as well as that any efforts to influence the process by dishonest means is likely to become public. Because the environmental authorities often have less power than many of the affected industries or their political partners, built-in transparency also protects them from pressure tactics from companies or other ministries.

- *List of participants.* While individual conversations can be private, policy makers should always publish a list of all groups and individuals with whom they spoke. This spotlights situations where parties with vested interests have flooded the process with their representatives. The list should also be reviewed for the opposite problem -- who is missing -- to ensure that all important stakeholder interests have been heard.

- *Explanation of decisions.* As decisions will always go against the wishes of some stakeholders, it is important that policy makers state publicly why particular decisions were reached and why they went against the stated interests of a particular stakeholder group. The process of simply acknowledging the opposing positions can do much to ameliorate resentment by these parties, as they can see that their views were considered.

Structured time line. Information from third parties plays a direct role in how policy makers view the environmental problem and the options for solving it. Unfortunately, these parties often use their information strategically, releasing only the bits that help their particular case. More often than not, such information is released in dribs and drabs, when additional support or refutation is needed for their case. This dynamic increases the difficulty of developing sound policies from the outset and can greatly delay the policy process. Stipulating deadlines for particular input can solve this problem, and re-establishes the policy maker as the party in control of the situation.

- *Data provision window.* Ministries should require that any data held by stakeholders and relevant to assessing the magnitude of the problem, the impacts on various parties, and options and impacts of solutions (especially on the choice of instruments) be provided within a certain time range. Data not provided would be ignored.

- *Policy comment window.* Subsequent to the release of the short-list of policy options, there would be a relatively short window for comments on these items, after which a final policy package would be chosen.

Unless both deadlines are strictly enforced, stakeholders will not take them seriously, and all of the previously existing gaming of the system will quickly return. Note these windows also set timelines for government officials to solicit this input from the less powerful groups most affected by the policies. Applying the same requirements to the government sends a strong signal in terms of equitable treatment for all parties in the process, as well as supporting a more rapid process of policy development.

Rather than full consensus, defining zones of agreement between parties, as well as clarifying the trade-offs among various options, may be sufficient to map out the refined policy framework. This type of information enables policy makers to make realistic assessments of the political barriers to action and the social implications of policy proposals.

Input from stakeholders then feeds back into the information compilation constructed during Phase 1, documenting the refined understanding of the problem. This allows refocusing of the Phase 2 "short-list" of policy options, narrowing the choices and identifying the appropriate flanking measures to implement with a particular EI to address the social or political barriers. Flanking measures commonly involve exemptions, deferrals, or transitional subsidies to help those groups (often the poor) most adversely affected by a policy change. Issues regarding international competitiveness often come up as well, with domestic industries arguing that they will be harmed by environmental controls not faced by their international competitors. Understanding the dynamics of the problem and the affected parties can expand the range of choices. For example, rather than exempt large domestic industries from important environmental policies as is often done, a solution might be to try to establish parity by ensuring imported products meet similar standards.

3.4   Phase 4: Policy implementation and evaluation

The policy implementation and evaluation phase involves moving from outreach and data gathering to choosing and implementing a final policy package. If the earlier phases have been completed well, a good deal of the rationale for the policy choice, and the outreach to affected parties, will already have been done. Exhibit 3.2 provides a simple template that can be used to compare the final options across key criteria. Again, the use of a matrix ensures that important data and impact categories are compared for each option. Each separate option generates two columns in the table. The first, "Option review" will provide very brief text summaries of the policy alternative. The second, "Ranking", provides comparative rankings that will make policy comparisons easier to do. Ranking methods can be changed to suit needs and preferences (e.g., use of numbers rather than high, medium low; or by weighting some criteria more than others). Similarly, evaluation criteria can be modified as well to better reflect the objectives of policy makers. This type of a comparison can be helpful in trying to decide amongst the final slate of options.

Exhibit 3.2

Policy ranking template

Policy parameter	Option review*	Ranking* (H,M,L)
Description		
Main policy		
Choices re: distribution of initial rights, ability to transfer, duration and caps		
Performance		
Environmental efficacy		
Complexity		
Cost of implementation and operation		
Anticipated side-effects		
Social: highly impacted groups (exposure, job loss, increased poverty)		
Short-term economic impacts		
Long-term economic impacts		
Trade and competitiveness impact		
Proposed flanking measures		
Feasibility		
Institutional capability to implement?		
Powerful opposition?		
Other factors of interest/concern		

*Each of the final policy options should have its own review and ranking columns.

Important aspects of the final choice of policy and on policy implementation are discussed below:

Choice of policy instrument

Deciding on the most appropriate new policy instrument given the baseline conditions, the problem to be solved and stakeholder feedback is the central decision. The option with the highest efficacy, lowest side-effects (or ones that are addressable through relatively simple flanking measures), and greatest feasibility given existing power and institutional dynamics is obviously the best. Most likely, no option will score the highest for each category, so trade-offs will be needed.

Flanking measures to mitigate severe effects

Where policy implementation is anticipated to cause undue hardships on segments of the population, transitional measures need to be built into the initial policy package. Possibilities include phasing in limits more slowly to avoid sudden changes in prices or access rights; exemptions for groups who face high costs but are de minimis contributors to the problem; or transitional subsidies to highly affected groups. Aside from the reduction in hardship, the flanking measures play an important role in mitigating political opposition to the new policy

Inter-institutional cooperation

Instrument choice will influence which relationships are most critical to establish/develop. EIs that bring in public revenues or solve problems for other ministries as well as protecting the environment offer immediate allies. Strong existing relationships between the government and certain stakeholders may tilt the policy choice in a particular direction and a common vision can be built into the policy directly.

Marketing

It is important to explain what policy package is being implemented, why it was chosen, and what steps are taken to ensure that this decision makes sense and incorporates the feedback from the various stakeholder groups. The basic explanatory data should be concise, easy to understand, and released at the same time as the policy package choice. Where decisions go against the expressed position of stakeholder groups engaged in Phase 3, it is important to recognize this disparity and to explain the reasons for the decisions being made. Follow-up is also needed to address questions and to provide continued updates of progress or resistance to the policies.

Monitoring and enforcement

Total quality management expert W. Edward Deming noted that if "we can't measure it, we can't manage it". Measurement is needed to evaluate progress, to determine when policy modifications are needed, and to learn from the existing applications so new applications are easier to accomplish. Both the environmental problem and the baseline conditions change over time; this can change the incentives faced by firms and resource owners. The more complicated a programme is to monitor and enforce, the less likely it is to succeed, especially in the developing world.

Though the details of monitoring and enforcement needs will be shaped by the specific policy package, these components need to be included in the policy package from the outset. In fact, where data collection does not require new authority, it is useful if the environment ministries begin collection even before successful policy implementation. Often data on the severity of baseline environmental damages or emissions can strengthen the power of the environmental interests to prevent policy derailment. Transparency is normally a great foe of vested interests.

EIs are often easier to measure than CACs, since simple-to-gauge metrics such as price of a pollution permit, tax levels, presence of performance bonds, etc., are clearly visible. Policy makers should plan to track relevant parameters over time and to make them public. OECD has developed useful guidance on evaluative criteria for economic instruments, which are mentioned below:[20]

– *Environmental effectiveness.* Are emissions levels or resource depletion rates falling? Are ambient concentrations in the surrounding environment declining? These are critical metrics to establish both baseline values and measurements over time. Unfortunately, even this basic data is often lacking.

– *Economic efficiency.* Are costs of emissions rights stable or declining? Are they less expensive than projected in advance by government or industry? These measures are easy to conduct for EIs. Falling values normally indicate that businesses are finding more efficient abatement methods. Are new abatement technologies entering the market? Are trades being actively used? Falling values with declining trades suggest either that new non-polluting options have emerged or that polluters are not purchasing required permits.

---

[20] OECD, *Evaluating Economic Instruments for Environmental Policy,* 1997, pp. 91-99.

- *Administration and compliance costs.* Has the public sector implemented an effective administrative oversight programme for the policies? How expensive is this to run relative to the value of trades occurring, emissions reductions realized, or anticipated cost of CAC programmes? How expensive are the administrative costs to the private sector relative to those normally incurred under a CAC approach? Are institutions cooperating to achieve the policy objective, or are efforts being blocked?

- *Revenues.* Are user fees sufficient to cover the full costs of providing particular public services? Are fees appropriately levied on different user groups? Are environmental taxes high enough to trigger appropriate price increases in the products/production processes of concern? Are revenues retained to support additional environmental protection efforts or diverted to the general Treasury?

- *Wider economic and social effects.* Are there noticeable (positive or negative) effects on employment, poverty, trade, competitiveness, growth, or rates of innovation that can be reasonably attributed to the environmental policies being evaluated? Where these impacts are negative, are they transitory or permanent? Can policy modifications mitigate the transitional dislocations?

Establishing policy credibility early on is critical if the affected parties are going to take it seriously. Maintaining strict control of the input process and timeline during the policy evaluation phase is a central part of this process, signalling that the ministry is open to outside information but will control how this information is being used. Credible and strong enforcement actions from the point of implementation is also critical. As with inviting information during policy development, the strong enforcement actions should also be supported with outreach and compliance support to help industries having trouble complying. However, unless violators are brought to task for failing to control their resource use or emissions, credibility for the programme and possibly the ministry overall can decline rapidly.

3.5 Summary

Solutions to environmental concerns will depend upon the particular situation, the problem as it has been defined, the structure and strength of institutions concerned, and the factional interests in a particular issue area. Exhibit 3.1 suggests the key questions to ask in order to establish a clear understanding of the barriers and drivers of policy change. Investing the time to evaluate these factors can greatly enhance the quality of the policies developed, as well as their ability to address potential impacts on poverty or trade. Strategic use of existing institutional capabilities can establish allies within the government that may be necessary to offset the potentially powerful interests of those benefiting from the lack of environmental controls. Careful explanation of the final policy choices, including a clear discussion of the severity of the problems being addressed and the steps taken to mitigate adverse impacts on specific groups can further help support the policy and weaken opposition. Finally, monitoring and enforcement systems need to be established from the outset in order to more clearly demonstrate both the severity of the problem and the potential benefits of the proposed solution.

4. Learning from Others: Case Studies, with Emphasis on the Developing World

Economic instruments have been applied in a wide range of countries to address an equally wide range of environmental problems. The following analysis attempts to make a general assessment about what instruments have worked effectively to address particular types of environmental problems, by examining a number of specific case studies. As in preceding chapters, the cases are grouped by the structure of the situation (e.g., controlling demand for use of publicly owned resources), and not by the environmental harm addressed (e.g., land degradation from grazing). Exhibit 4.1 gives an overview of what has been tried for particular sectors, using data derived from a number of multi-country surveys. Factors associated with success, partial success, or failure of these applications are noted. While sometimes overlooked or played down in other assessments, the failed EIs have been included in this report in as much detail as the successfully applied EIs. This was done with the view that as much can be learned from the failures as the successes, thus facilitating improved instrument choice or policy structure in future applications.

Summaries of the case studies are presented in this chapter. A more detailed review of some of the case studies can be found in Annex C, according to the availability of information.[21] A range of sources has been used, and the information available on the particular EI application varies widely across case studies. The analysis contained in this report was contingent upon the availability of data and information, which was far from comprehensive. The conclusions drawn are those of the author. Using an expanded and more detailed library of case studies in the future could help refine and expand the generalizations that are made here. Despite this limitation, the systematic analysis of cases helped to identify and clarify many of the general issues on EIs presented in chapters 2 and 3. The case studies clearly show that if certain baseline conditions do not exist or are not met, EIs are bound to fail.

The emphasis of this chapter is on the developing world, though EIs are of course also beneficial in the developed world. This focus reflects the desire to identify solutions to the severe environmental problems that many of these countries face with their limited resources of all types. Despite severe environmental degradation, developing countries generally depend on their environmental and natural resources for economic development. Policy dislocations that threaten people's survival or generate public protests from subsistence populations and political resistance due to unequal wealth concentration are very real concerns. Other concerns include limited funding, weaker institutional capacity and lower capacity for environmentally-related research and development.[22] Many of these countries have existing CAC environmental regulations in place, but they are frequently not enforced.

---

[21] The template structure differs slightly between Exhibit 3.1 and Annex C. The structure in Exhibit 3.1 focuses on gathering information in a structured way, from which to narrow policy options. Because Annex C contains descriptions of policies that have already been implemented, some modifications in structure were needed to integrate what is known about the historical policy drivers, implementation, and effectiveness. Most of the core information in both templates, however, is the same.

[22] Based on Rietbergen-McCracken and Abaza, 2000, p. 7.

4.1   Overview of instrument choice from EI surveys

Exhibit 4.1 presents data on many EI applications gathered from multi-country surveys. The instruments are grouped in a matrix that combines their functional objective with the resource areas being protected. The number of areas to which economic instruments have been applied is quite extensive, underscoring the flexibility of these policy approaches to meet a wide range of important needs.

Depending on the point of the matrix, different aspects of policy and institutional structures dominate. For example, to control access to resources, the EIs often focus on licensing or auctioning of rights. How these initial rights are distributed and maintained is of great importance in the type of behaviours that will then emerge. Enforcing terms of contract relies heavily on a functioning judicial system, whereas efforts to encourage efficient use of resources and infrastructure via user fees require financial institutions within a country to operate effectively. Policy applications tend to be fairly similar within a functional area (i.e., down a column). In contrast, there are few linking factors within a single resource area that cut across multiple functional areas (i.e., across a row). This finding supports the decision to group EIs according to their function throughout the report.

One crucial point to highlight is that the efficacy of EIs in all of the five functional areas is reduced when there are baseline subsidies to environmentally harmful activities or behaviour. These subsidies counteract the positive effects of economic instruments and should be phased out whenever possible.

Exhibit 4.1
Common applications of EIs by resource area

Resource Area	Functional Area				
	Control access to resource	Recover direct costs plus fair return	Curb emissions	Enforce contract terms	Subsidize preferred behaviour
Description	Control extraction/use rates at locations, so resource is not depleted haphazardly.	Recover direct costs of goods/services provided from beneficiaries; obtain fair return on sale of public resources/assets.	Force beneficiaries to pay for their use of land, water, and air quality.	Provide financial incentives to insure contract terms, especially with regard to clean-ups and accident prevention, are enforced.	Provide financial assistance to encourage a shift to preferred products or productive methods.
Resource Area					
Minerals and Energy	-Licensing, auctions -Tenure reform	-Rents, royalties, bonus payments -Excise fees	-Pollution taxes -Marketable permits -Effluent charges	-Reclamation bonding -Litigation -Decommissioning or waste management fees -Tax breaks for pollution controls	-Government-financed health, safety, environmental functions -Subsidized access to energy for the poor
Water	-Licensing withdrawals -Municipal control of fresh water flows -Marketable withdrawal rights	-User fees, for water and wastewater treatment -Privatization of infrastructure construction, operation	-Effluent charges, varying by volume or constituents of discharge -Fees on non-consumptive water withdrawals -Permitting of dischargers	-Fines and litigation -Environmental liability insurance	-Tax breaks for installation of pollution control equipment -Subsidized access to water for the poor
Timber	-Licensing, auctions -Tenure reform	-Cutting fees -Access charges		-Reforestation bonding -Fines and litigation for improper cutting, reforestation	-Tax breaks for reforestation -Reduced property taxes on timberlands -Subsidies for watershed protection during timbering -Subsidies to protect urban greenery

Functional Area

Resource Area	Control access to resource	Recover direct costs plus fair return	Curb emissions	Enforce contract terms	Subsidize preferred behaviour
Fisheries	-Marketable quotas -Regulatory access controls -Terminate subsidies to fleet construction	-Purchase and rental costs of ITQs -Fishery landing fees -Fishery permit fees	-Petrol fees for water pollution cleanup -Fisheries management revolving funds	-Fines and litigation for non-compliance with fishing permits	-Public payments for fishing fleet retirement -Municipal development of efficient fish processing capabilities
Transport	-Toll roads, sometimes with peak rates -Access fees	-Tolls -Gasoline taxes -Vehicle weight charges	-Gas guzzler taxes on inefficient vehicles -Regulation/ inspection regimes for vehicle efficiency, emissions	-Liability insurance requirements for accidental spills -Environmental fines, litigation for accidents	-Excise tax reductions/exemptions for preferred fuels (lead-free petrol; biofuels; renewable energy)
Agriculture and Grazing	-Permitting, licensing for grazing on public lands -Tenure reform -Auctioning of grazing rights -Fees for development of agricultural land	-Implement full cost recovery for public sector agricultural support, insurance programmes	-Excise taxes on fertilizers, chemicals -Regulation of discharges to air and water -Discharge fees on manure		-Public funding of soil conservation, sustainable farming practices; training -Subsidies to protect biodiversity, particular cropping methods
Habitat/Bio diversity Protection	-Regulation/restrictions on development in certain regions -Tenure reform -Taxes on destructive activities (e.g., gravel extraction)	-Fees on recreational access or individual extractive activities (e.g., sport fishing, hunting) -Fees on ski lifts	-Tradable development permits allowing rights to be used in less sensitive ecosystems	-Environmental fines, litigation	-Subsidies for maintaining high water levels -Tax breaks for donation of development rights to a land bank
Air Quality	-Licensing or regulation of air discharges often forms baseline control	-Recovery of government regulatory costs via user charges	-Targeted pollution charges -Purchased pollution permits (may or may not be transferable)		

Functional Area

Resource Area	Control access to resource	Recover direct costs plus fair return	Curb emissions	Enforce contract terms	Subsidize preferred behaviour
Nuisance (e.g., noise)	-Higher fees for particular airports encourage fleet redeployment	-Earmarking of fees for noise abatement programmes in affected community	-Noise charges	-Performance bonds	
Waste management	-Licensing/privatizing waste management sites	-Collection fees for waste pickup -Tipping fees at municipal dumps -Waste taxes per unit of hazardous waste managed	-Taxes on nuisance products (tires, batteries, motor oil) to finance recovery system. Rates often higher on more toxic items -Deposit/refund systems (cans, bottles, car hulks) to encourage diversion, recovery -"Pay-as-you-throw" charges per bag, encouraging participation in recycling programmes	-Trust funds for closure and post-closure management of dump sites -Environmental liability insurance -Environmental fines, litigation	-Disposal fees often cross-subsidize recycling and household hazardous waste diversion -Basic trash pickup often free due to health concerns

Source: Compiled by Earth Track, Inc. commissioned by UNEP, 2004, using data from OECD (1999), Panayotou (1998) pp. 189-197 and Huber, Ruitenbeek, and Seroa da Motta (1998).

Note: Reform and/or removal of baseline subsidies to environmentally detrimental activities provides additional leverage to achieving environmental improvement.

The following sections discuss the application of economic instruments to the main functional objectives shown in Exhibit 4.1. These are:

- limiting access to publicly owned resources;
- recovering reasonable fees from resource users;
- managing government sales of publicly owned natural resource assets;
- reducing pollutant loadings to the environment; and
- subsidising the transition to more sustainable alternatives.

Multiple cases for each area are included when available, with cross-cutting insights highlighted where possible.

4.2   Limiting access to publicly owned resources

Overuse of natural resources through open and unrestricted access by many parties is a recurring environmental problem, often referred to as the "tragedy of the commons". The policy challenge is not only to constrain resource use, but to do so in a way that does not require an unreasonable level of government oversight (which is often impossible to provide). When over-exploitation is the result of pressure from subsistence populations, reforms in land tenure have been a successful solution. When over-exploitation is the result of larger and sometimes more international users, more formal property rights approaches such as tradable permits have been applied. These approaches have been fairly successful because they give the authorized parties a direct financial stake in the resource base. In turn, this creates a self-interest in sustainable harvest rates as well as in direct monitoring to prevent poaching. When data on the resource base is poor, or there is no power to take action against poachers, the EIs have been less successful. Similarly, the more mixed the resource base (e.g., one species of fish versus multiple species caught together), the more difficult it is to establish clear rights.

Tenure reform: Mankote Mangrove, St. Lucia [23]

One of the more successful examples of tenure reform involves the Mankote mangrove. Mankote comprises the largest contiguous tract of mangrove in St. Lucia, and 20 per cent of the total mangrove area in the country. Widespread and uncontrolled charcoal harvesting from the trees put the mangroves into severe environmental decline. The loss posed a significant threat to the many ecosystem services mangroves provide, including maintaining coastal stability and water quality, serving as a fish breeding and nursery ground, trapping silt, and providing important bird habitat. Most of the charcoal was harvested by subsistence populations. These people were extremely poor and had no legal right to any use of the publicly owned mangrove resources. They did not have obvious alternative employment should their access to the mangroves be cut off due to resource depletion or degradation.

To address the core problem of protecting the mangrove, the subsistence users were organized into a collective and granted communal tenure rights to charcoal extraction. For the first time, they had a direct stake in the sustainability of the resource base. The group tenure also gave each individual harvester an incentive to monitor his peers to ensure cutting regimes were being properly followed. Technical training in effective ways to manage cuts was provided, as well as periodic monitoring of the overall mangrove health (as measured by tree size and number of new stems). Longer-term efforts to reduce the economic pressure on the mangrove were implemented using job training programmes and the development of a hardwood forest outside of the mangrove. This last element has been of limited success. Finally, in addition

---

[23] See Annex C for a complete write-up of this case study.

to securing the tenure of the charcoal harvesters, the programme worked to prevent threats to subsistence harvesting from large scale development or fishing by establishing Mankote as a nature reserve.

By modifying property rights, St. Lucia (in large part due to efforts of the Caribbean Natural Resources Institute, a regional NGO) has been able to protect the Mankote Mangrove and all the ecosystem services it provides. Mangrove depletion has been stopped and tree cover is now increasing, all without displacing jobs. Despite the overall success, the case does have some problems. First, the process has been extremely long, taking more than 15 years. Many resources at risk would not survive such a long policy gestation period. Second, risks to the mangrove remain. For example, the tenure is granted through a letter from the Deputy Chief Fisheries Officer; case study materials do not indicate the degree of protection provided by such a letter. Threats from outside developers remain, and challenging the validity of the tenure rights would seem an obvious tactic. Even intensive development at the borders of Mankote could fragment ecosystems sufficiently to reduce the viability of the area. Policy planners need to consider the resources they are trying to protect holistically in order to identify potential threats before they become too large. Finally, there is little information on how the new tenure holders will constrain internal growth of their group to ensure harvest pressures remain sustainable.

Protecting fishery resources using transferable quotas (multiple countries)[24]

Fisheries have long been a commons problem, as fish dwell in unmanaged ecosystems accessible by many countries. Historical controls to address this problem have focused on restricting access. Nationalization of 200 miles of coastline by most countries helped reduce fishing pressure for a while, by curbing access from foreign fleets. However, problems remained even with domestic fleets, and access restrictions to threatened fisheries have been common. Continual technical improvements in fleets made each boat a more effective vessel for harvesting fish. In addition, large subsidies to fishing-related capital equipment (e.g., subsidized loans for boats) and operations have created a massive overcapacity of vessels. The World Bank has estimated that during the 1990s, annual subsidies were equal to between 20 and 25 per cent of global fishery revenues.[25] The combination puts many fisheries at substantial risk of depletion.[26]

Over the past 30 years, many countries have implemented market-based approaches to ration access to fisheries.[27] Variously called Individual Transferable Quotas (ITQs) or Individual Fishery Quotas (IFQs), the rights allow the holder to catch a specified proportion of the total allowable catch (TAC) each year. The TAC represents the central government's estimate of how many pounds of a particular fish species can be sustainably harvested.

The theory of ITQs is clear. Where there once was unlimited and free access to fish, users must now be licensed. They can space out their catch more regularly without fearing that others will overuse the resource, enabling them to fish more when prices are high, increasing their profits. The aggregate catch of the vessels is limited, ensuring sufficient fish survive to

---

[24] See Annex C for a complete write-up of the Chilean and South African experiences with ITQs.

[25] Milazzo, 1998.

[26] UNEP, 2002a and 2002b.

[27] While some countries such as Chile have adopted ITQs recently, other nations have used this approach for more than 20 years. New Zealand, Australia, and Iceland, for example, first deployed ITQs in 1982, 1984, and 1984 respectively/(Smith and Vos, 1997, pp. 71, 74).

rebuild stocks. Finally, each license holder has an incentive to ensure other vessels do not fish illegally, since this reduces the available catch for license holders and depresses the value of the licenses on the spot market, which existing quota holders can sell.[28]

OECD reviewed 31 fisheries across six countries using some variant of this approach and concluded that catch levels were maintained at or below catch limits in 24 cases. In 23 cases, the permits also improved the cost-effectiveness of, and profits within, the fishery. While overall employment generally fell, part-time and seasonal jobs were often replaced by more stable, year-round work.[29]

However, the success of the programmes seems to be dependent upon some key criteria. Information is extremely important; if the TAC values are too high, transferable permits simply exhaust the resource more efficiently. OECD noted that there were at least temporary declines in fish stocks within 24 fisheries.[30] In Chile, there are significant concerns that TAC figures are not as precise as they need to be. In the Netherlands (sole and place fisheries) and Norway (cod fishery), ITQs failed to halt the increase in catch because license holders found that the state was still shutting entire fisheries down even if individual quota holders had not met quotas yet.[31] As a result, quota holders continued to have a "race to fish" to exhaust their catch limits first before access was closed off. This seems to be evidence of a basic problem in the way these countries calculated the TAC, but the error has eliminated many of the environmental and ecological benefits of the economic instrument.

Errors in TAC values may not all be technical. Regulators in South Africa have been under continued and intense political pressure to increase the TACs, irrespective of the environmental cost of doing so. This pressure probably exists in most countries, and where institutions are weak or corruption rife, limits can be manipulated for private gain. For example, catch quotas are often based on landing statistics. Many fishermen destroy catch at sea to produce acceptable landing numbers making it impossible to reconcile the landing statistics with the actual pressure placed on marine ecosystems.[32] Leal suggests that a post-landing spot market, allowing fisherman to purchase excess quotas, may alleviate this pressure to some degree.[33]

High-grading is another common problem, where smaller fish are discarded (and often die) at sea in order to maximize the value of the catch that is officially landed. Differential landing taxes, with higher levies on bigger fish, in theory could make fishermen neutral with regards to the maturity of their catch.[34] However, the monitoring needed to accurately set and implement such taxes could be quite large. Thus far, applications of ITQs have steered clear of multi-catch fisheries, another complication of fishery management. They have instead licensed a single species. While bundled ITQs covering common mixtures of species could be created, implementing it in practice is difficult as by-catch is likely to vary by region.[35] Adler (2003) notes that ITQs, by eliminating the race to fish, allow more carefully targeted capture methods, thereby reducing degree of by-catch. However, some by-catch will remain, and adoption of improved capture methods is unlikely to be universal.

---

[28] Sutinen, 2001, p. 4.
[29] Wallis, 1999, pp. 117-121.
[30] Ibid. p. 117.
[31] Sutinen, 2001, p. 3.
[32] El Serafy, 2002.
[33] Leal, 2002, p. 21.
[34] ibid. p. 24.
[35] ibid. p. 21.

Politics are an additional factor to address, well illustrated by the case of Chilean fisheries. The country has three main fishery interest groups: northern fishermen, southern fishermen, and artisanal fishermen (who use small boats and stay close to shore). Political manoeuvring of the northern and southern fishery corporations focused on access to the initial fishing rights, and ways to use this property for competitive advantage. The ultimate decision to auction long-term fishing rights helped ensure more open access to outside parties. The artisanal interests have opposed the ITQs with the argument that the small boats, and the communities they support, would be frozen out of their livelihood. As a result, fisheries covered by the ITQs still allow open access for artisanal interests. This free access to fisheries may be one reason that the number of artisanal vessels has grown by 27 per cent between 1994 and 1998. Efforts to set up a separate class of ITQs for the artisanal fishermen is now under consideration.

Growth in the use of the ITQs in Chile has been small, with applications to only four fisheries covering roughly 1 per cent of total landings. The rest remains under a complicated and not particularly effective system of access controls, fleet limits, and equipment restrictions. Ownership of ITQs is highly concentrated (two groups control 75-90 per cent of the northern harvest), and there have never been fines levied for infractions of the ITQ rules. There has also been some evidence of pricing collusion. These factors underscore the need for credible monitoring and enforcement even for EIs, as well as addressing baseline issues such as market power. Nonetheless, the programme does incorporate a number of useful elements, such as caps on ITQ ownership by any single party and a 10 per cent annual depreciation of quotas, ensuring there will be regular auctioning and pricing of the rights. Some fisheries have undergone stock recoveries, and many fishing operators say they have been able to improve the quality of their final products, plan more effectively to meet higher price demand periods, and reduce social conflict with their workers by offering more regular work schedules.

Summary

Licensing and property rights reforms can be powerful tools to curb over-utilization of natural resources. However, careful attention to programme structure is needed in a number of areas. Setting appropriate parameters for the EIs being used requires that accurate and timely information on the overall health of the resource to be protected is available. These figures are subject to intense political pressure, so ensuring that the source of the data is insulated from political influence is important. Monitoring of compliance can be done in part by utilizing the interest that existing rights holders have to curb cheating. However, as the fisheries example illustrates, when the geography of the resource is widely dispersed, supplemental monitoring is needed. Monitoring of trading rights is also needed in order to create an efficient market for exchange of rights and to remind existing rights holders how much their licenses are worth.

Over-utilization of resources by subsistence groups around the world can be addressed through modifications in tenure rights (individual or group). However, this approach is not without risks: "many local communities will choose the immediate return of exploitation before long-term sustainability".[36] Careful attention to the range of rights being granted is necessary, and subsequent monitoring and adjustment are needed if the resource base continues to diminish.

---

[36] DFID, 2002, p. 22.

4.3   Recovering reasonable fees from resource users

The public sector invests hundreds of millions of dollars to bring services to the populace of many developing countries: electricity, drinking water, and wastewater treatment are examples. Similarly, government owned natural resources comprise an asset of the state, owned by its citizens. There are strong arguments to be made for supporting cost recovery from beneficiaries for both consumptive (e.g., harvesting firewood, grazing) and non-consumptive (e.g., recreation) use. Full-scale asset sales of non-renewable resources (be they oil reserves or government owned enterprises) create a different set of problems and are addressed in a later section.

Because both the services and the resources have measurable economic value, and can be expensive to make available, pricing access through the use of EIs is a common solution. As shown in Exhibit 4.1, user fees have been applied in nearly every resource area. Not only does cost recovery bring in revenues that can allow the government to continue to provide the services or to manage the asset base, but it also sends more accurate price signals to users, encouraging more appropriate resource consumption. Finally, because extending municipal services to poor areas (water, sewer, electricity) often comes years after the initiation of services to the wealthy or middle class, appropriate cost recovery can ensure adequate funds are collected to facilitate these second round extensions.

Despite the logic behind cost recovery, there is a widely held belief that many of these municipal services should be free. As a result, implementing charge systems is often politically difficult. And, as shown by the case studies below, charge systems based on politics rather than economics often fail either to collect sufficient revenues or to protect the resource base.

The goal of these EIs should be to recover appropriate fees from the beneficiaries, providing subsidies only to the poor; to charge higher amounts to users who force the system to incur higher costs; and to recover sufficient revenues from all paying customers to ensure the sustainability of the enterprise.

Management of forest reserves in Botswana

Alarming deforestation rates were evident in some parts of the forest reserves in Botswana, owned commonly by the State. Existing CAC approaches were not working. These included restrictions on any cutting in forest reserves without prior permission, the use of local committees to develop conservation-minded use plans, and the ability of the Ministry of Agriculture to declare regions "planning areas," thereby instituting cutting restrictions. A payment scheme, including payment of fees and royalties, was also of limited success. Fees were set at a flat rate, regardless of the diameter of the trunk (i.e., no linkage to value or board feet). This encouraged harvesting of the oldest trees first, removing many of the large anchor trees that help maintain biodiversity and wildlife habitat, and that should normally be left even after cutting. Trees less than 35 centimetres in diameter had no royalties at all, also contributing to excessive removal. Royalties were paid only on the tree trunk, valuing other parts of the tree effectively at zero.

Widespread over-harvesting has led to increased tree litter and fire risks. The tree litter problem is compounded by the high damage rates and inefficient processing associated with inexpensive stumpage (overall yield is only 18 per cent). Finally, elephant herds in some forests such as the Chobe knock down many trees, exacerbating the fire risk. With prime wood so inexpensive, there has been little incentive to spend time on salvage.

Fee reforms have been proposed to address most of these problems. Fees are to be higher, recovering a fuller set of the costs associated with timber activities, including government oversight and fire suppression/prevention. The royalty rate for damaged stock is lower, to encourage salvage harvests, though it is not clear from existing data how the government will ensure honest reporting on this issue. In addition, the royalty rate will cover the entire tree, not just the trunk, to encourage better usage. Finally, to curb problems of trying to oversee many small cutters, concessions have been limited to large firms.[37] The reforms make sense in terms of the type of incentives they provide to wood harvesters. Unfortunately, available information does not provide details on whether even the new, higher fees are sufficient to change behaviour, nor on how the government will enforce the new charges. Finally, one critical aspect of resource extraction does not seem to be addressed: how reforestation and sustainable cutting practices will be encouraged.

Grassland pricing reform: Philippines[38]

Pasture Lease Agreements (PLAs) for ranchers to graze cattle on public lands have existed for decades in the Philippines. The lease terms last 25 years, and are renewable for another 25. Prices for these rights have been extremely low (roughly US$0.30/hectare/year). As a result, a relatively small group of people has gained control over much of the public grasslands for the 50-year lease period. The ability to shift cattle to new pastures they control has also reduced the incentive for sound management of the pastureland, and led to land degradation in many parts of the country. Although existing rules require ranches to file annual operating plans as well as a management plan every eight years, there is virtually no government follow-up to ensure plans are actually being implemented. This is the result of insufficient funding as well as difficult terrain to oversee.

To improve land management, the Department of Environment and Natural Resources (DENR) has been working for years to raise the fee to a more reasonable level. The target fees were estimated based on a study of the market value of grazing rights, and finally implemented in 2001. The target fees were set in three tiers, reflecting differing grassland quality, with the lowest being 24 times the current fee. Despite some evidence that even this fee was too low, and the fact that 80 per cent of the surcharge could be used to correct degradation on the leases, the ranchers have fiercely resisted the increase. A number have refused to pay the higher rates, a situation the DENR had not been prepared for. As a result, fee collection has stopped entirely on these parcels. Also, a top government official, without any advance consultation with the DENR, pledged to cut the grazing fees sharply during a visit to the region. This pledge triggered suspension of the fee pending further clarification from the DENR.

Though the rationale for charging market rates for grazing makes a great deal of economic and environmental sense, DENR has been unable to overcome local political opposition. As a result, the grasslands remain under great threat, and additional resources that the higher fees would have brought in are not available to stem the damage. Existing ranching practices are unsustainable, and current regulations on management reporting and planning by ranchers are not enforced. In the face of such opposition regarding fee levels and enforcement, auctioning of rights could have offered a better solution.

---

[37] Reitbergen-McCracken and Abaza, 2000.
[38] A detailed write-up of this case study can be found in Annex C.

Water charge for river basin access: Brazil[39]

A number of Brazilian rivers were facing increased degradation and water scarcity. The rivers cross both state and international borders, so solutions required a coordinated response across many government agencies. In addition, there were hundreds of affected users who needed to be brought into any environmental management system created. River Basin Committees formed the local management units responsible for protecting the rivers, but had little power to actually do so.

In their first iteration, the committees were ineffectual because they had little formal power to influence river usage and protection. Inadequate stakeholder outreach in the initial stages has been identified as one source of this weakness, though resistance to new fees by users probably also played a major role.

A comprehensive water law, passed in 1997, addressed many of these shortcomings. The law adopted river basin management through the river basin committees, and broadened the mandate of these committees to more explicitly address river recovery and to finance their activities through water fees. Most of the recovery plans included water user fees that varied depending on the amount used and pollution content of the activity. The institutional focus on water was also sharpened with the creation of a Water Resource National Council (CNRH) and an executive federal water agency (ANA) both directly linked to the Ministry of the Environment. However, considering the vast territory and complex hydrologic structure of Brazil, the new water management system was conceived to be gradually implemented and to provide great autonomy to the committees.

Water charges were envisioned under the water law to have three purposes: to demonstrate to the population that water was an economic (not a free) good; to encourage rational water use; and to obtain funding to finance the programmes in the River Basin Management Plans.[40] Thus far, existing applications of fees seem to focus primarily on financing River Basin Management Plans. Pricing to encourage rational use has not been implemented. In addition, critical issues regarding institutional arrangements, universality of chargeable uses, autonomy of basin committees and charge revenue allocation criteria still dominate the debate and are postponing the rapid implementation of water charges.

ANA is promoting several experiments in establishing water fees in an effort to speed up fee roll-out across the country. As a result, charges are already in place in the Paraíba do Sul River Basin and in design in other three basins. (Charges in the Ceara region are also in place, but pre-dated the current law). The charge setting has been made after a broad and extensive consultation with affected parties within the Committee. The belief is that this piece-meal approach will help the most workable approaches to evolve, thereby avoiding problems that arose in other countries where implementation failed due to a weak regulatory framework and institutional capacity.

With early efforts to improve management of Brazilian river basins dating back to the late 1970s, the Brazilian system has been slow to develop. National legislation granting the authority needed to manage and finance river basin management came twenty years later. Furthermore, six years after the passage of the enabling legislation there are still few charge systems in place and those that are in existence are immature. It is still too early to evaluate

---

[39] A detailed write-up of this case study can be found in Annex C.
[40] Campos and Studart, 2000, p.151.

how successful the system will be in gradually introducing efficiency, equity and ecological considerations. Earlier federal involvement to establish a common authority for water management might have helped speed the process up. Similarly, more direct involvement to ensure Basin Committees have an adequate technical basis to measure water consumption and degradation, and to set equitable charges that encourage water conservation and protection, could help reduce delays and challenges to charge implementation today.

Summary

The logic of charging users for what they consume is hard to challenge. However, as these cases illustrate, implementing these systems is nearly always difficult. Existing charges, if there are any, tend to be very low and often do not rise with inflation. This provides existing parties with windfall gains from their access to under priced resources. It also means that they will fight strongly to block or delay any efforts to institute more rationale charge structures. Engaging stakeholders early, as well as clearly explaining why the charges are needed and what they are for, may help in some cases. What may be more effective would be to provide clear and timely data on which sub-groups are paying for the resources, which are not, and show the implications of those not paying on the services for all. This type of information can at least divide the user base so that a portion will support more effective fees. Similarly, where fees do exist, it is quite important to enforce them fairly and extensively, especially when they are first implemented. If non-payment is ignored, it can quickly go from a minor problem to a major one.

As illustrated with the case of grazing in the Philippines, auctioning licenses to use a particular resource can sometimes substitute for a user fee. Although auctions will not work for cost recovery on government owned or built infrastructure, they can be very helpful for applications where there is little fixed infrastructure and the users can be quickly changed. Not only do auctions bypass the need to guess what the appropriate fee might be, but they quickly remove the government as the main point of conflict. Rather than complaining about fees that must be paid, the auction winner now owns a right that does not necessarily require any additional payments to the government, but does encourage conservation due to its resale value. Overcoming political resistance remains the largest factor to consider when planning a cost recovery charge-scheme.

4.4   Managing government sales of publicly owned natural resource assets

Small scale harvesting of natural resources can often be addressed using fee structures, once the political hurdles to implementation are addressed. Large-scale asset sales are a very different situation and raise two critical problems: ensuring assets are sold at a fair price, and protecting windfalls from being squandered by public officials. These challenges are addressed in turn below. Examples include tenders for large timber, mining, or energy concessions; or the privatization of government owned enterprises or infrastructure such as nationalized oil companies or electrical generating stations. The market value of the assets is so large that there are often attempts to divert these resources to public officials or their supporters through graft and corruption. These problems are most severe in resource rich countries with weak central governments and an absence of fiscal transparency.

Receiving fair value on asset sales (multiple countries)

Research has highlighted the problems of operating under corrupt governments. For example, in some countries, the revenues from logging concessions in the forestry sector will often go to corrupt government ministers. In other cases, where almost all forests are public land, forest concessions are commonly used as patronage to reward political allies. Even if the regime changes, however, elected legislators will often block efforts to ban logging in particular areas or to increase logging fees. Or even when corrupt behaviours appear to be gone, proper pricing and management of timber resources still remain a problem. Concessions are often long-term (roughly 20 years), and often become highly concentrated within a few hands. High profits from concessions then allow owners to build expansive empires in other areas of the economy. In turn, the power and funding that these empires have created has enabled their owners to further co-opt and manipulate the public sector oversight mechanisms that should be protecting the general interest of the public.

Addressing corruption is not easy, and is not limited to any particular regimes: patronage is common in many democracies as well as dictatorships. However, market-based approaches - primarily auctions and stock market flotation - may provide a viable solution in some circumstances. Furthermore, data compiled by Transparency International suggests that countries with high levels of globalization tend to be the least corrupt.[41] Oil and gas lease auctions provide one model for ensuring competitive sales. To be competitive, auctions must have a sufficient number of bidders, bidders must be unable to collude, and government officials must actually award the lease to the highest bidder.[42] Finally, there must be an independent authority to collect bid-related payments and royalties.[43] These can be most easily met in conditions of transparency: sales are publicly announced and described; they are open to domestic and foreign bidders alike; and the winning bids are published. Tracking of funds through independent auditing agencies is also necessary to prevent diversion of resources.

Stock market flotation on an established market can help control fraud through the listing requirements firms must meet before being allowed to sell shares in these markets. These entail disclosure of all kinds of information on assets owned, management structure, sales, compensation of officers, etc. In contrast, private sales within a country or stock flotation on

---

[41] Marc Levy, 2001, data and research section, pp. 227, 300-302.

[42] Doug Koplow and Aaron Martin, 1998 pp. 6-19.

[43] The Extractive Industries Transparency Initiative is an effort spearheaded by the British Government to establish reporting guidelines on the costs and benefits of resource extraction activities around the world. Because reporting is voluntary, it is not clear how effectively it will garner increased transparency in this important area. See http://www.dfid.gov.uk/News/News/files/eiti_core_script.htm for more information.

markets without strict oversight and accounting requirements are both at much higher risk for fraudulent diversion of assets to interested and politically-connected parties.

Natural resource concessions are an illustration of the importance of integrated flanking measures as well. Receiving a fair bid for resource exploitation rights becomes far less meaningful if the mining, timber, or oil company leaves an environmental disaster in its wake. Thus, the use of financial assurance mechanisms such as third party performance bonds, is an important supporting policy.

Protecting gains for the long-term: The Alaska Permanent Fund[44]

An equally challenging aspect of these large asset sales is ensuring that the resulting proceeds are not squandered. This is a problem that often does not get sufficient attention, as the statistics are fairly bleak. States heavily dependent on mineral revenues often turn out poorly in the UNDP's Human Development Index; this trend is far worse when oil dependence alone is examined.[45] Even if not diverted to corrupt officials, the funds are all too often used to prop up the government budget, leaving the general populace with little to show for the tens of billions of dollars in wealth extracted from their lands.

A notable exception is the US state of Alaska. Concerned with just this outcome, the state instituted a Permanent Fund in 1976. Established by a State Constitutional Amendment, the fund is fairly well protected from political machinations. The Fund receives at least 25 per cent of all mineral lease rentals, royalties, royalty sale proceeds, federal mineral sharing payments, and bonuses received by the State. Applying the calculation before consideration of any costs or expenses ensures that the amount to be deposited into the permanent fund is much more difficult to manipulate. The amendment also created an independent corporation (the Alaska Permanent Fund Corporation) to oversee the Fund, independent auditors, and strict investment and fund disbursement guidelines. Investments are widely diversified, and only interest (not principal) may be paid out to fund beneficiaries. Essentially, this is a State endowment fund, but one that has been very successful in converting non-renewable oil wealth into a permanent, diversified income stream for the state and its citizens. The Fund provides a powerful model for resource-rich states or countries around the world.

Summary

Ensuring a fair return on the sale of valuable government assets is an extremely important task, yet one that can be quite difficult. For many poor nations that have substantial natural resource endowments, the revenues from selling resource concessions or government owned enterprises can make the difference between a cash-starved government and a solvent one. Environmentally, market-based prices also help curb the incentive to deplete resources for extremely low value uses. Institutional transparency and independence are of utmost importance in this area, a prerequisite to being able to achieve competitive sales. International efforts, such as the Extractive Industries Transparency Initiative out of the UK may help. Export credit agencies and the multilateral lending institutions are also often involved with these large scale sales or development efforts, and should be forced to give greater attention to ensuring appropriate checks and balances with the sales or privatizations, as well as monitoring during the subsequent operating period. Finally, existing economic structures for managing endowment funds can be easily adapted to the public sector to ensure that at least a portion of the natural resource wealth is protected and diversified for the benefit of the population.

---

[44] Information obtained from the Alaska Permanent Fund website (www.apfc.org) in September 2002.
[45] Ross, 2001, p. 7.

4.5   Reducing pollutant loadings to the environment

Although pollution to air, water, and land occurs in many industries, pollution intensity (emissions per unit produced, or per dollar of sales) varies widely. Even within a single industry, there are widely varying emissions levels depending on the technology employed and the sophistication of management. Command and control regulations are commonly employed to bring emissions down, but tend to be fairly rigid, setting maximum loadings or stipulating the installation of specific capital equipment. CAC approaches often allow industries to pollute for free below the statutory limit. Economic instruments such as emissions fees and pollution permits can achieve many of these same objectives more effectively. They can also work in parallel with CACs, helping to allocate the abatement needed to meet the CAC target more efficiently. As with the other EIs, instrument design is important. For example, maximum loadings (set by regulation) may be established on a regional basis, with trading constraints or zones set up to ensure that no population group receives dangerously high emissions as a result of trading.

Nutrient trading at sewage treatment plants: New South Wales [46]

When nutrients are discharged en masse to waterways, they generate algae blooms which, in turn, use up all of the oxygen in the water killing other life. As a result, treatment of nutrients is a central job of sewage treatment plants before the wastewater can be released to the surrounding environment.

Beginning in 1996, three sewage treatment plants owned by the Sydney Water Corporation in the South Creek area of the Hawkesbury-Nepean River initiated a nutrient trading system. Under the regime, the three plants are allowed to trade portions of their nutrient discharge allocations, so long as the aggregate loading limit is not exceeded. The process of intra-firm trading within a set geographic area is called a "bubble," since a single limit or bubble applies to the river, rather than to a single plant.

The trading scheme set target reductions by 2004 of 83 per cent of the phosphorous and 50 per cent of the nitrogen. Oversight is provided by the local regulatory body. The programme is generally considered a success. After three years, there were substantial reductions in nutrient loadings, at a much lower cost. The cost savings, estimated at 37 per cent as compared to each plant meeting uniform requirements, come primarily through capital cost savings. Capital investments to curb nutrients can be concentrated in one or two plants, versus all three; and upgrades can be more closely timed with normal capital replacement than would have been possible under a uniform standards approach. Monitoring data was not complete in the review, and the overall impact of the programme on environmental quality in the receiving waters was not available. This is an important data gap since detrimental effects of excessive loadings can be localized within receiving waters (causing "hot spots" of environmental damage). Applications of tradable permits of any type need to evaluate the likelihood and impacts of such hot spots in order to be sure that the overall environmental objectives of the programme are met. In addition, plans to expand the trading system to more parties, and to non-point sources of nutrients as well, have been under discussion for some time, but have not been implemented yet.

Lead trading in the USA [47]

During the 1980s, restrictions to the use of lead additives in petrol were set up in the US, with

---

[46] Kraemer, Interwies, and Kampa, 2002, pp. 250-251.
[47] OECD, 2001, pp. 21-22.

the ultimate aim of phasing out use of leaded petrol entirely. To ease the process of adjusting to the more stringent standards, especially for smaller suppliers, a lead trading system was instituted in 1983. It was slated to operate during the five-year transition period to the new lower limit of 0.1 grams per gallon, and allowed refiners and importers to trade lead reduction credits in order to meet limits. The lead reduction credits were to be created when suppliers of leaded petrol achieved lead levels lower than those required by the new limits. The system allowed for both internal "trading" (i.e. flexibility) for an individual supplier, as well as external trading between suppliers. Beginning in 1985, refineries were allowed to "bank" lead credits for use in future years.

The general consensus is that this programme has performed successfully, reducing costs by approximately US$ 250 million per year, though use patterns of leaded petrol may have been altered somewhat. Among the factors to which its success has been credited are: a clear definition of rights and obligations; a predefined time over which the programme would operate; a homogeneous product with a clear definition for all market participants; and low transaction costs in implementing trades.

Emission fees in China [48]

In an attempt to curb pollution from factories, the government set up an emissions fee. As is true in most countries, these fees constituted business expenses, and were deductible from taxes. Given common Chinese corporate tax rates of 33 per cent, this means that for each dollar in fees, roughly one-third remained in the firm as a tax-shield, reducing taxes that would have been paid on other net income. In an effort to accelerate installation of pollution controls, the Chinese set up a rebate system, whereby 80 per cent of the fee collected would be returned to the enterprise for investment in pollution controls. Thus, from this original dollar in fees, 33 cents comes back through reduced tax burden and 80 cents comes back in a (ostensibly tax-free) rebate, for a total of US$1.13. Thus, paying the pollution fees offered a net gain of roughly 13 per cent. The example clearly illustrates the creation of perverse incentives because of an imperfect design.

This perverse incentive made firms not wish to invest in pollution controls, lest they lose the privilege of paying emissions fees to earn a quick 13 per cent return on their money. The ability to do so was the result of a lack of political will or capability to ensure rebated fees were invested in pollution controls as required rather than spent elsewhere in the business. The government replaced fee rebates with loans in an attempt to solve the problem; however, enforcement has been weak. In addition, the funds from the 20 per cent of fees not returned to the enterprise goes to the local environmental authorities, and this has supposedly given them an interest in maintaining funding through maintaining emissions. Were rebates actually put to use in upgrading pollution controls, this may not have been such a bad policy. It underscores once again the importance of matching policy designs with institutional capabilities.

Summary

Economic instruments such as emissions charges, trading, and permits have a solid track record around the world for reducing the costs of compliance. The most extensive trials have involved air pollution. Measurement of markets and trades, and enforcement all remained important supporting elements to the programme. Furthermore, as illustrated in the China example, programme design, including subsidies, need to be carefully matched against the monitoring and enforcement capabilities in order to create the desired incentives for industry.

---

[48] Blackman and Harrington, 1999, pp. 18-21.

4.6   Subsidizing transition to more sustainable alternatives

Encouraging environmentally sustainable practices and technologies through government subsidies is commonly raised as a suggestion. There are many options for how subsidies can be provided, ranging from direct grants to low interest loans, government indemnification to tax subsidies. The instrument that is chosen, as well as the behaviours for which the subsidy is earned, have important implications for the types of behaviour that is encouraged. The more efficient subsidy programmes provide no support for private activity unless it is successful in achieving the desired end-goal. For example, the United States used to provide investment tax credits (allowing firms to reduce US$1 of taxes owed for each US$1 invested in the desired industry) for new investments in renewable energy. These subsidies flowed even if the investments failed and never produced any electricity. Current forms of this subsidy provide tax breaks on a per unit of electricity produced only. Thus, while encouraging wind power, for example, the government has not taken on any of the technological or market risks of the new power sources.

The case studies below illustrate other complexities associated with trying to accelerate transition to environmentally preferable alternatives. Too often, when subsidy targets are poorly defined or politically influenced, financial resources are provided with little or no environmental gain. In other cases, targets may be proper, but the number of parties too large to provide subsidies to all. In such circumstances, regulation of damaging behaviour may be a more appropriate strategy.

Timber discounts for reforestation: Colombia, Brazil and Venezuela

In an effort to encourage good reforestation practices, timber policies in Colombia, Brazil, and Venezuela all charge a tax on wood consumption, except when the harvesting is offset by equivalent reforestation.[49]   Recognizing that there are insufficient resources to oversee reforestation directly, these countries have chosen to forego revenues from timber sales so long as the cuts are properly replanted. The programmes have generally failed due to fees that are very low and poorly enforced. Especially in frontier regions, monitoring is difficult.[50] A lack of institutional capacity and/or will yields a situation where neither the environmental or the fiscal goals are being met. Forestry fees that were historically collected in Brazil were often completely used up to finance administrative overhead in the oversight agencies rather than the environmental purposes for which they had originally been intended.[51]

Leveraging existing subsidies for environmental protection: Soil conservation in the Dominican Republic

In the El Naranjal watershed in the Dominican Republic, US AID funds provided subsidized credit to participating farmers adopting soil conservation measures. Initial adoption rates were quite high (90 per cent in 1985), yet by 1990, only half of the farms continued to practice the conservation measures, as the subsidies had stopped. Where further subsidies are expected, farmers may actually delay rational conservation measures in order to wait for the payment. The follow-on project of US AID recognized that the farms were already receiving tremendous benefits in the form of subsidized irrigation water. This second project tied continued access to subsidized water to proper adoption of soil conservation measures. The result has been substantial use of conservation techniques without additional direct subsidies.[5]

---

[49] In contrast, timber policies in the US, while they are subsidized, aim for forest users to pay for the timber and for reforestation.
[50] Seroa da Motta, 1998, p. 7.
[51] Seroa da Motta and Reis, 1994.
[52] Lutz et al., 1994, p. 291.

Even where existing subsidies cannot be removed due to political constraints, they can be leveraged to ensure adoption of more sustainable practices. There could be many potential applications of this principle throughout the developed world. For example, aggregate subsidies to the agricultural sector within the OECD alone are US$362 billion per year.[53] Were access to these programmes restricted only to farms practicing environmentally sound growing techniques, the environmental benefits would be enormous.

Seed capital: Externally financed development of premium bulb markets in Turkey[54]

Transitional subsidies work best when the need really is short term, and the newer approaches are quickly shown to be viable in the marketplace. Indigenous propagation of threatened Turkish bulbs provides one such example. To offset an accelerating loss in national wild stocks, the World Wildlife Fund decided to fund demonstration projects on the propagation of domestic bulbs as a substitute. The WWF project also benefited immensely from the fact that domestic bulbs were also increasingly being specified in international trade contracts as the knowledge about dwindling wild stocks grew. Using contracts with growers, plus capitalization funding to finance the initial purchases of plant stock for the participating families, the Fund was able to jump-start a more sustainable domestic industry. In this situation, project returns were sufficient to make the enterprises viable. In addition, adoption of the new approach was widespread because it required little change in existing routines of participating families and increased their economic gains.

Renewable portfolio standards in the US: Bringing market forces to transitional subsidies

Renewable Portfolio Standards (RPS) provide a powerful model for how transitional subsidies can be provided in a well-targeted, efficient, and dynamic way. Like cap and trade systems for pollution permits, the RPS approach blends CAC and EI approaches. Governments set a predetermined target for renewable energy sources as a percentage of total electricity purchased within the state. Electric utilities must generate eligible power directly or contract with third parties to meet these targets. Some states allow trading of renewable energy credits (REC) to create a more liquid market for meeting RPS requirements. Non-compliance with renewable energy targets is normally met with large fines of twice the REC rate, which are applied automatically on the utility. Funding for the more expensive renewable energy (RPS power is normally at a slight premium) comes through surcharges on residential customer bills.

The efficiency of the policy arises from the fact that the renewable energy sources must compete with each other to win renewable energy supply contracts. Although these energy sources will often be purchased at a premium to conventional electricity, the size of the premium is bid down by the competitive nature of the market. Technical improvements in the generation of renewable energy can be expected to bring down the unit cost of this power over time; and these improvements will be felt almost immediately through reduced premiums within the RPS. The US Energy Information Administration has argued that even with some premium, RPS may still be cost neutral in terms of the electricity cost overall. This is because the additional supply source helps reduce both the price volatility of, and the demand for, natural gas. The resultant drop of roughly 0.5 cents/kWh in gas prices roughly offsets the purchase premium on renewable fuels.[55] `

---

[53] Upton, 2002, p. 4.
[54] CBD, 1998, pp. 3,4.
[55] EIA, 2002; Chen et al., 2003, p. 2.

RPSs are currently in use in 11 US States (Wiser, 2003), and can work in either a regulated or a deregulated electricity market. As with the fishery ITQs, policy structure matters in achieving an efficient and effective policy. Setting percentage targets to be met with renewable energy is a first important parameter. Normally, initial targets are quite low, rising over time. This ensures that there are no cost-shocks to the system, but that the market participants can begin to provide alternative power over a reasonable planning horizon. Which energy sources are eligible is a second critical issue to address. Allowing sources that are not really renewable can undermine all of the environmental objectives the policy is attempting to achieve.[56] Similarly, eligible sources are normally newly constructed rather than existing, as the goal of the programs are to encourage new renewables capacity rather than subsidize existing plants. The large and automatic penalties are also very important in ensuring that the programme works.

Other factors that improve programme functioning include compatibility in allowable renewables with surrounding states (so generators can feed multiple states) and to ensure that all retail sales are subject to the same RPS requirements. Finally, programme stability is important. Research by the US Department of Energy suggests that the ability to enter into long-term power supply contracts under an RPS is an important factor in bringing prices down.[57] Predictability in the mandated levels and eligible sources is also important for efficient market development. Where states do not have clear information on when the RPS mandates end, financing renewables projects has been more costly and more difficult.

Summary

Subsidies to "good practices" can help realign research and market forces in ways that accelerate the transition to improved products or production methods. These approaches are especially important where parties causing the damage have very little purchasing power of their own (as in subsistence farmers) or where the environmental benefits accrue primarily to parties very different from those bearing the direct costs of behaviour change (as with many biodiversity-related issues). However, the provision of subsidies in no way assures that the desired environmental end-goals will be obtained. Because the political interest in obtaining public subsidies is always large, careful evaluation of proposals are needed. Assessment of whether markets can produce the changes without new subsidies, whether existing subsidies to detrimental practices can be removed or made conditional on adoption of sustainable practices, should be considered. Structuring payments so they are limited in scope, reach only the population sector that needs it, and only for a transitional period of time is important. Using competitive forces within the transitional subsidies to ensure that technical improvements gradually bring down the unit cost of the subsidized activity is another useful approach.

Transitional payments to negatively affected groups should be managed in the same way as any other dislocated worker if possible, e.g., by using unemployment insurance. Even where transfer payments may make sense, such as with biodiversity, unless these payments are carefully structured and monitored there is a real risk that some in the local community will take the transfer payments and continue to poach the resources that threaten the long-term viability of the resource trying to be protected.[58]

---

[56] Energy sources that have environmental detriments can include biomass, landfill gas, animal wastes, and hydroelectricity. Biomass can be an issue if it is not sustainably produced. Subsidies to landfill gas recovery undermine materials recycling (see Koplow, 2001). Animal wastes can further tip the scales in favor of large scale monoculture farming, worsening market conditions for sustainable approaches. Finally, hydroelectric dams often have impacts on local river ecosystems.

[57] Wiser, 2003.

[58] UNEP, Economic Instruments in Biodiversity-Related MEAs, 2004.

4.7   Conclusions

EIs have been applied to solve a vast range of resource and pollution problems, affecting all environmental media. Understanding the structure of the problem to be solved as well as the baseline conditions, and choosing an instrument most suited to address that structural problem, can greatly increase the likelihood of success. However, the case studies have also illustrated that instrument choice alone is not enough.   Policies must be developed holistically, paying careful attention to exactly what behaviours are being rewarded.   For example, charging premiums for existing renewable energy will do little to encourage new and more technically competent supply. Levying fees based only on the trunks of trees but not on branches will provide an incentive to waste all but the largest part of the timber.

In addition, political considerations remain at the core of many of the policies implemented, even to the detriment of the environment. Where political opposition is strong, even the most logical argument for controls, user fees, or new requirements will be heavily challenged. Including political strategies in the design and implementation of policy to confront opposition should be the norm. Better information on the true "winners and losers" can help. So too can strategies that replace government oversight or rent collection with marketable rights or privatization (or private operation) of government infrastructure.

Monitoring and enforcement are also critical to environmental protection, without which the effectiveness of many EIs can be quickly eroded. Charcoal harvesting from mangrove forests relies on the eyes of all license holders in order to stabilize the resource base. And accurate information is of course necessary to support policy implementation. For example, in the fisheries sector, without reliable data, use of ITQs may worsen depletion rather than ameliorate it.

The case studies also demonstrate that when policy design does incorporate these elements, EIs have performed well in practice in a variety of resource areas. In the United States, Rewable Portfolio Standards have begun to expand their use of competitive sources of renewable energy.   The Mankote mangrove forests are recovering, as are some Chilean fisheries. Not only can EIs facilitate cost-effective reductions in emissions or resource use, but they can also help ensure adequate returns on resource sales to third parties, and the protection of those returns for the use of future generations. The following chapter discusses the lessons learned and suggests opportunities for further developing our knowledge and understanding of the use of economic instruments for environmental protection.

5. Lessons Learned and Opportunities for Further Research

Economic instruments are powerful tools for achieving environmental goals at a lower cost, and often more effectively than many of the CAC policies now in place. Additionally, the ability to use EIs together with existing CAC approaches is of great benefit. The efficiency improvements associated with EIs must nevertheless be balanced against the constraints posed by current policies, institutional capabilities and factional interests.

This paper has developed a number of tools to help policy makers structure disparate data more efficiently in order to refine their understanding of the problem they are trying to solve, to more quickly identify appropriate policy options, and to tailor these options to local conditions.

There are a great number of instruments and they are applied to a wide range of environmental problems. They are, however, generally used to achieve some mixture of three main goals:

1) using property rights to redress problems that contribute to pollution or poor stewardship of resources;
2) establishing and enforcing prices for resources consumed and environmental damage associated with production; and
3) subsidizing transition to preferred behaviours.

The paper has focused particularly on the functional objectives of EIs rather than the type (e.g. permit, tax, deposit), with a view to providing a more intuitive understanding of which tools are appropriate under particular circumstances. The evaluation of case studies has shown that there are many commonalities in the tools applied to achieve the main objectives (see Exhibit 4.1), even across very different resource areas. For example, the main aim in establishing a system of property rights is to manage access to resources in order to control resource extraction or use. Within the cost recovery area, EIs are structured to achieve three distinct, but often interlinked objectives: recovery of the direct costs from beneficiaries to provide public goods or services; receive just compensation for the sale of valuable public assets; and establish financial charges and accountability for environmental harm.

Subsidies are commonly applied to accelerate the development and adoption of clean technologies or more sustainable resource use patterns, relying either on government provided financial assistance or through government run programmes. However, subsidies create distortions of their own and are often very difficult to end once they are implemented, so they should be used with great care. It is important to ensure for example that subsidies are clearly targeted, only applied in the short-term, and do not end up exacerbating the problems instead solving them.

Section 5.1 summarizes important insights into the policy-making process, including the four main phases of policy development, and highlights some of the recurring challenges that become apparent when reviewing EI applications around the world. Section 5.2 summarizes a number of patterns in how EIs have been used around the world that emerged, providing an insight for those addressing current problems. The final section identifies a number of areas that would benefit from additional research in order to further improve the ability of policy makers to identify and implement appropriate EIs around the world.

5.1   Insights into the policy-making process

Establishing a viable policy package involves four main phases: 1) assembling information in a structured way, 2) identifying a short-list of the most suitable policy options, 3) engaging stakeholders to help refine policy choice, and 4) implementing and evaluating the policy. While the theoretical benefits of particular market-based (EI) control approaches are important, practical consideration of the status quo, including institutional strength, existing policies, and stakeholder power dynamics, will have enormous influence in deciding the most viable policy approach. The key issues to consider as policy development proceeds are outlined below. These are intended to provide guidance for developing more effective policy, but should not be viewed as insurmountable barriers. In fact, EIs can help solve many resource use problems even in countries with high poverty and less effective supporting institutions.

Baseline conditions are critical

It is important to spend the necessary time defining the problem, identifying factional interests, and evaluating past attempts to address the problem. The information base should then be assembled into a structured template from which an initial set of policy options can be proposed and developed.[59] At this point, a process of stakeholder involvement and feedback should be established to gather additional information and to revise assessment of the problem and the proposed range of solutions accordingly. Care should be taken to avoid seizure of the process by vested interests, as this can slow down the policy process and redirect policy in directions that are less effective and/or more expensive.

Current institutional and economic capabilities need to be realistically assessed. If instrument choice or structure can be adapted to, or compensate for, identified institutional weaknesses, this would generally be the preferred course of action; trying to address environmental problems concurrently with trying to improve baseline conditions may risk failure. If the weaknesses preclude any policy solution, there may be no alternative but to implement institutional reforms, particularly if the environmental problems are severe. Such reforms would obviously require a broader coalition than just environment ministries.[60] Policy design should be commensurate with the problem to be solved, avoiding taking overly complicated measures.

Alternative measures to address identified problems should also be considered. If there are gaps in baseline institutions, then implementing CACs may have also the same problems as EIs. In such circumstances, because EIs can operate at a more decentralized level, they may be preferable.

Reaching political agreements

It is important not to underestimate the challenge of reaching agreement. Establishing a process of stakeholder involvement is crucial in order to understand the terrain and to provide interested parties with a mechanism to be heard. However, it does not necessarily lead to consensus, and the process needs to be managed strategically. Clear definition of timelines and structuring of the stakeholder process can speed up development of policies. To be effective, the environment ministry needs to enforce its timeline in a consistent manner.

---

[59] See Exhibit 3.1, as well as completed templates in Annex C.
[60] Where institutional gaps exist, it is important to clearly identify these gaps, and to prioritize which are most important for addressing pressing environmental problems. Both financial and technical support is often available from international agencies to assist in this process.

Many of the case studies evaluated in the report indicate the length of time often needed for policy gestation, and the fact that there is still no guarantee of end result. Development periods of more than ten years were not uncommon, and there was little evidence that longer periods of consensus building were linked to a greater chance of policy success.

Political challenges also continue even after policy instruments have been chosen. Technical challenges in establishing appropriate tax/charge levels are mitigated to some degree by the ability to modify them over time based on observed market reactions, reducing the pressure to get the initial formulation perfect. However, imposing realistic fee levels on established resource users or polluters can be difficult. In addition, creating and supporting new markets (e.g., for pollution permits) can be challenging, especially where there is no history of strong markets in other commodity areas.

Gathering data on the resource base, which parties are damaging it, and how the costs of that damage are spread among other users and the surrounding population, should take place early in the process. This information can help to justify policy proposals, as well as divide potential opposition groups by identifying which ones are harmed by the status quo.

Implementation is the beginning of the game

Monitoring and enforcement are the lynchpins to achieving environmental progress. Expectations on how seriously to take the new policies will be set early, so policy makers need to set the right tone. Instituting a mechanism for third parties to bring suit can offset weaknesses in governmental environment enforcement capabilities.

Disclosure and transparency are necessary tools to ensure the EI is working, and to help offset continual pressure from affected stakeholders to water down or co-opt the policies. Provision of key information on environmental quality and existing subsidies as early in the process as possible will support subsequent policy implementation as well as the initial policy choice.

It is quite common to attempt to achieve political consensus via payments or other subsidies to affected parties. However, providing subsidies to transitional behaviours in favour of sustainable practices should be used sparingly since they create distortions of their own and are often very difficult to end once they are implemented. Rather, subsidies should focus on protecting the poorest sectors of society from any severe impacts of the change. This could be done with:

- A focus of payments for poverty alleviation; transitional payments (e.g., the introduction of environmentally-sound technologies); and situations where social benefits greatly exceed private benefits (often where existence and bequest values of a resource are high and flow to more technically-advanced societies).[61]
- Transitional payments should be decoupled from any activities causing environmental damage, and should be time limited.
- Support for subsistence sectors should also be decoupled from environmentally damaging production if at all possible and shifted to subsistence consumption.
- Where central governments cannot be relied upon to provide direct subsidies to the poor, pricing mechanisms (increasing block rates, subsidies flowing only to basic subsistence foodstuffs) should be used instead.

---

[61] Existence value represents the economic value that people place on a resource for just knowing it exists, even if they do not anticipate using it directly. Bequest values are similar, but attempt to measure the value people place on being able to pass on a particular resource to future generations. These values often apply to resources that are irreplaceable, such as natural wonders or biodiversity.

– Where transitional subsidies are used to accelerate development and implementation of new technologies, look for market-based structures such as Renewable Portfolio Standards to accomplish the goal. These will often be more dynamic and more efficient that grants or tax subsidies.

5.2　Generalized policy solutions

The choice of the most appropriate policy is influenced by a wide range of factors including environmental laws already in place, the power and technical capability of ministries involved, and the broad economic conditions within the country. It is therefore important to recognize that there is no precise formula for deciding when to apply a particular EI. However, certain patterns as to when and under what conditions EIs have been successfully employed were evident from the case reviews. The prevailing circumstances of a resource/emissions problem, and the generalized policy solutions that have been used are described below. In many cases, modifying some of the flanking measures or policy implementation variables (see Annex A) can help tailor the generalized solution to meet the specific conditions in a given country. The findings also indicate that instrument choice is driven far more by the problem structure than by the resource area, as described below.

Overuse of natural resources. Property rights-oriented approaches, such as granting or selling specific groups the rights to access or develop particular resources, can work well in situations where current use patterns are depleting the resource base. Where informal access patterns by local users are codified, subsistence livelihoods can be protected while concurrently providing much improved direct incentives to manage the resource for the long-term. Even in more international markets, permits that differentiate commercial and subsistence users can help achieve a balance between resource protection and employment. If consumption must be curbed, buy-out or phase-out of the existing de facto rights is a possibility.

Industrial pollution, disparate technologies. Where emissions of pollutants of concern result from many different industrial sources, there are likely to be widely varying costs to abate the pollution. In these circumstances, there are often large efficiency gains from imposing pollution taxes, fees, or tradable permits relative to mandatory standards under a CAC regime.

Industrial pollution, standard technology, few producers. Where there are few producers, all relying on similar production technologies, disparities in control costs are generally much lower. These circumstances suggest minor gains from trading alongside potentially large oversight costs to create a market. CAC regulatory approaches may be the more efficient option.

Known damage thresholds. Where regulators have a good sense of the point at which emissions cause health problems or ecosystems begin to fray, tradable permits are often the best choice. Caps on emission/extraction can be set in advance, either based on absolute values (e.g., tons of salmon that can be caught) or on relative values (e.g., percent of total allowable catch), allowing markets to allocate the rights efficiently. Policy adjustments should be made on a regular basis to adapt to changing conditions or errors in the initial caps.
Government owned enterprises. The objective with government owned enterprises is to institute pricing that achieves full recovery of costs through user fees, but with a rate design

that protects the poor for subsistence consumption needs. Attempts to cover the costs of the enterprises often bring to light their inefficiencies, increasing pressure for improved management and governance structures. The combination of revenue collection and increased organizational efficiency can be a powerful help to governments. Improved cost recovery can make system upkeep easier, with resultant improvements in efficiency of resource use, and more feasible system extensions, often with associated equity benefits such as providing electricity or sewage services to poorer regions for the first time.

Government owned enterprises in highly politicized environments with substantial rent diversion. Government owned enterprises in natural resource areas face difficult challenges in preventing corruption (large cash flows, often poor transparency) and in instituting appropriate environmental controls (government litigation against itself is uncommon). In such cases, both the fiscal and environmental well-being of the country can be served through privatising the enterprise. This can be done either through a direct sale, or by floating a portion of the company on the stock market in the developed world. The listing requirements provide important leverage to facilitate disclosure and transparency, necessary prerequisites to overcoming factional interests benefiting from the status quo.

Transition to new technology. Moving an existing market structure to one that includes more environmentally-friendly approaches involves multiple challenges: developing a technology that works; convincing firms to use the technology; and ensuring that the final product can actually be sold. Some market shifts that mostly require changes in management (e.g., soil conservation on farms) can often be accomplished by making the continuation of existing subsidies contingent on the adoption of sustainable practices. Where new equipment must enter the marketplace but is still more expensive, policies should reward initiatives once they are sold. Thus, rather than subsidizing research and development (R&D) or plant construction for wind power, a subsidy per unit of wind power purchased in the market would be provided. Competitive contracting approaches, such as Renewable Portfolio Standards, can be used to ensure that even this subsidy is as small as possible.

Long-term programme support should come from within. External resources (e.g., from NGOs or international agencies) can support initial research or training. However, they should not be relied on to operate the programme, as the entire effort will be at risk when funding priorities change. Because many EIs also raise revenue through licensing fees or permit sales, such programmes have the potential to be self-sustaining. Diversion of collected funds for other purposes (such as to general government spending) can negate this policy benefit.

5.3 Next steps

This report suggests a structure for identifying, evaluating and applying EIs to environmental problems, especially in the developing world. UNEP will support case studies to test and further develop this tool. Additional knowledge in a number of core areas would make these systems even more effective:

Case study library. Much can be learned by studying the application of EIs across resource areas, as well as by examining the variation in EIs developed to address similar problems (e.g., ITQs in fisheries) in multiple locations. Past case study compilations are of limited value since they do not provide a standardized structure for data reporting, but rather summarize applications anecdotally. By establishing a centralized repository for standardized reporting on EI applications, understanding of why policies are or are not successful can be greatly expanded.

EIs and poverty alleviation. There seems to be a high correlation between high levels of poverty, low environmental quality and poor governance; thus, the opportunities for policy confluence could be substantial. Consideration should be given to how EIs can be applied to existing situations in order to protect the environment more efficiently while also alleviating poverty. A current initiative on Environmental Fiscal Reform, led by a number of OECD donor agencies and with participation of developing countries and intergovernmental agencies, is a first step in this direction.

Barriers to increased transparency in government interventions affecting environmental quality. Improved information on fiscal and subsidy policies would undoubtedly yield many options for saving money and improving the environment. A better understanding of what the barriers to achieving that increased transparency are might help remove them.

Institution building. Opportunities for improving the core baseline conditions in countries with critical global natural resources should be assessed, despite the very large challenges. Biodiversity hot spots are one clear example. In such situations, building institutions that can effectively carry out environmental protection regimes, including those incorporating EIs, is imperative.

Most importantly, efforts will have to be made to improve the capacities of policy makers and other stakeholders to assess the value of EIs and to design and use them in an efficient and effective way. Capacity building activities will have to be conducted on the basis of needs assessments, taking into account the priorities and circumstances of individual countries. UNEP is planning to develop training manuals and to conduct workshops in developing countries, in cooperation with other institutions and agencies, to further these processes.

Glossary and Abbreviations

CAC	command and control
de minimis exemptions	regulatory exemptions for firms or individuals that contribute only a very small amount to a particular environmental problem
EI	economic instrument
ESI	Environmental Sustainability Index
IFQ	individual fishery quota: a right of a firm or individual to use fishery resources.
ITQ	individual transferable quota: a right assigned to or bought by, a firm or individual to use a particular resource. Most commonly used in reference to fisheries.
NGO	non-governmental organization
OECD	Organization for Economic Cooperation and Development
PLA	Pasture Lease Agreements, giving owners long-term grazing rights to particular pastures (Philippines)
PPP	polluter pays principle
R&D	research and development
REC	renewable energy credits: transferable credits to demonstrate compliance with RPS targets.
RPS	Renewable Portfolio Standards are government stipulated targets for the percentage of total electricity within a political jurisdiction that must be met from approved renewable generating sources.
TAC	total allowable catch: the total tonnage of a particular fish species that is deemed sustainably harvestable based on monitoring of fishery health.

References

Adler, Jonathan, personal communication, 21 May 2003.

Arntzen, Jaap. *Economic Instruments and the Southern African Environment: Synthesis of Experiences of Five SADC Countries,* University of Bostwana, September 1999.

Blackman, Allen and Harrington, Winston. *Using Alternative Regulatory Instruments to Control Fixed Point Air Pollution in Developing Countries: Lessons from International Experience,* Resources for the Future Discussion Paper 98-21, March, 1998 p. 6.

Borregaard, Nicola and Sepulveda, Claudia. *Institutional, Political and Technological Lock-Ins to the Introduction of Economic Instruments in Chile,* Centro de Investigacio y Planificacion del Medio Ambiente, November 1998. Prepared for the "Fifth Biennial Meeting of the International Society for Ecological Economics," Santiago de Chile, 15-19 November 1998.

Borregaard, Nicola. *Transferable Fishing Quotas in Chile: Case Study in the Design and Use of Market Based Instruments for Resource Policy.* Santiago, Chile: Centro de Investigacion y Planificacion del Medio Ambiente, October 2001, draft.

Campos, J.N.B and Studart, T.M.C. "An Historical Perspective on the Administration of Water in Brazil," *Water International,* V. 25, No. 1, pp. 148-156, March 2000.

CBD Secretariat. Secretariat of the Convention on Biological Diversity. "The Use of Economic Instruments Under the Convention on Biological Diversity," prepared for the UNEP Working Group on Economic Instruments, March 2002.

Chen, Cliff, David White, Tim Woolf, and Lucy Johnston. *The Maryland Renewable Portfolio Standard: An Assessment of Potential Cost Impacts,* Prepared for Maryland Public Interest Research Group by Synapse Energy Economics, Inc., 27 March 2003.

Convention on Biological Diversity. "Design and Implementation of Incentives Measures," Conference of the Parties to the Convention on Biological Diversity, 4th Meeting, Bratislava, 4-15 May 1998. Published 1 February 1998.
UNEP/CBD/COP/4/18.

Damania, R. "Political Competition, Rent Seeking and the Choice of Environmental Policy Instruments," *Environmental and Resource Economics,* vol. 13, pp. 415-433, 1999.

DFID. Department for International Development - United Kingdom, Directorate Generate for Development - European Commission, United Nations Development Programme, and The World Bank. *Linking Poverty Reduction and Environmental Management: Policy Challenges and Opportunities,* Consultation Draft, January 2002.

El Serafly, Salah. "Memorandum: Issues of Development and Distribution," 10 March 2002.

Esty, Daniel and Porter, Michael. "Ranking National Environmental Regulation and Performance: A Leading Indicator of Performance," in *The Global Competitiveness Report 2001-2002.* NY: Oxford University Press, 2001.

Godard, Olivier. *Strategic Guidelines for the Design and Implementation of Domestic Transferable Permits,* (Paris, France: OECD Working Party on Economic and Environmental Policy Integration), 19 June 2001. ENV/EPOC/GEEI(1999)13/FINAL.

Grace, Bob and Ryan Wiser. "Renewable Portfolio Standards: Background and Analysis for New York State," NYSERDA, 2 May 2002.

Hafner, Othmar. "Working Paper: The role of corruption in the misappropriation of tropical forest resources and in tropical forest destruction." Transparency International, 23 October 1998.
http://www.transparency.org/working_papers/hafner/ohafner.html on 4/16/2002.

Hahn, Robert. "The Impact of Economics on Environmental Policy," AEI-Brookings Joint Center for Regulatory

Studies, Working Paper 99-4, May 1999.

Huber, R.ichard M., Ruitenbeek, Jack, and Seroa da Motta, Ronaldo. *Market Based Instruments for Environmental Policymaking in Latin America and the Carribean: Lessons from Eleven Countries.* World Bank Discussion Paper No. 381, 1998.

Kitamori, Kumi. "Domestic GHG Emissions Trading Schemes: Recent Development and Current Status in Selected OECD Countries," in *Implementing Domestic Tradable Permits: Recent Developments and Future Challenges,* OECD, Paris, 2002, pp. 69-104.

Kraemer, Andreas, Eduard Interwies, and Eleftheria Kampa. "Tradable Permits in Water Resource Protection and Management," in *Implementing Domestic Tradable Permits: Recent Developments and Future Challenges,* OECD, Paris, 2002, pp. 250-251.

Koplow, Doug. "Evaluating Subsidies for Landfill Gas to Energy Programs," National Recycling Coalition, 2001 http://www.earthtrack.net/earthtrack/library/MethaneReport.PDF

Koplow, D.oug and Dernbach, John. "Federal Fossil Fuel Subsidies and Greenhouse Gas Emissions: A Case Study of Increasing Transparency for Fiscal Policy," *Annual Review of Energy and the Environment,* 2001, 26: 361-389.
http://www.earthtrack.net/earthtrack/library/Fossil%20Fuel%20Subsidies%20and%20Transparency.pdf

Koplow, Doug and Martin, Aaron. *Fueling Global Warming: Federal Subsidies to Oil in the United States,* prepared for Greenpeace, June 1998.
http://archive.greenpeace.org/~climate/oil/fdsub.html

Leal, Donald R. Fencing the Fishery: *A Primer on Ending the Race for Fish.* Political Economy Research Center, 2002.

Levy, Marc. "Corruption and the 2001 Environmental Sustainability Index," in Global Corruption Report 2001, data and research section, Transparency International, pp. 227, 300-302.

Lipper, Leslie. FAO, personal communication, 3/9/02.

Lutz, Ernst; Pagiola, Stefano; and Reiche, Carlos. "The Costs and Benefits of Soil Conservation: The Farmers' Viewpoint," *The World Bank Research Observer,* vol. 9, #2, July 1994, pp. 273-295.

Macinko, Seth and Bromley, David. *Through the Looking Glass: Marine Fisheries Policy for the Future,* Final Report to the Pew Charitable Trusts, 22 September 2001.

Mavrakis, Dimitrios and Konidari, Popi. "Classification of Emissions Trading Scheme Design Characteristics," *European Environment,* 2003, vol. 13, pp. 48-66.

Milazzo, Mateo. Subsidies in World Fisheries: *A Reexamination,* Washington, DC: World Bank. Discussion paper #406, April 1998.

OECD, Vos, Hans B., Barde, Jean-Philippe, and Mountford, Helen. *Economic Instruments for Pollution Control and Natural Resources Management in OECD Countries: A Survey.* Working Party on Economic and Environmental Policy Integration, 6 October 1999. OECD, Paris, 1999.
ENV/EPOC/GEEI(98)35/REV1/FINAL.

OECD. *Evaluating Economic Instruments for Environmental Policy.* Paris, 1997.

OECD. *Environmentally Related Taxes in OECD Countries: Issues and Strategies.* Paris, 2001.

OECD. *Domestic Tradable Permits for Environmental Management: Design and Implementation.* Paris, 2001.

OECD. *Implementing Domestic Tradable Permits: Recent Developments and Future Challenges.* Paris, 2002.

Pagiola, Stefano. "Economic Analysis of Incentives for Soil Conservation," September 1998, World Bank. Paper forthcoming in *Using Incentives for Soil Conservation,* eds., Sanders, D.W. et al., Science Publishers, Inc.

Panayotou, Theodore. *Instruments of Change: Motivating and Financing Sustainable Development,* London: Earthscan Publications Inc., 1998.

Pearce, David. *Levelling the Playing Field: Environmental Policy and Competitiveness,* forthcoming.

Reitbergen-McCracken, J. and Abaza, H. *Economic Instruments for Environmental Management,* Earthscan Publications Ltd., London, UK, 2000.

Ross, Michael. *Extractive Sectors and the Poor.* Oxfam America, October 2001.

Seroa da Motta, Ronaldo and Reis, Eustaquio. *The Application of Economic Instruments in Environmental Policy: The Brazilian Case,* Workshop on the Use of Economic Policy Instruments for Environmental Management, OECD/UNEP, Paris, 26-27 May 1994.

Seroa da Motta, Ronaldo. *Application of Economic Instruments for Environmental Management in Latin America: From Theoretical to Practical Constraints,* technical meeting, Sustainable Development in Latin America and the Caribbean: Policies, Programs, and Financing, Oct. 30, 1998, Washington, DC. Unit for Sustainable Development and Environment, General Secretariat, Organization of American States, Washington DC.

Smith, S. and Vos, H.B. *Evaluating Economic Instruments for Environmental Policy. Paris,* France: OECD, 1997.

Stavins, Robert N. *Experience with Market-Based Environmental Policy Instruments,* Washington DC: Resources for the Future, November 2001. Discussion paper 01-58.

Sterner, Thomas. *Policy Instruments for Environmental and Natural Resource Management,* Resources for the Future Press, Washington DC, 2002.

Sutinen, Jon G. Testimony before the Subcommittee on Oceans and Fisheries of the Senate Committee on Commerce, "Hearing on S. 637, the Individual Fishing Quota Act of 2001," 2 May 2001.

Upton, Simon. "What Should World Leaders Focus on at the Johannesburg Summit," OECD, Paris, 11 February 2002.

UNEP. *The Use and Application of Economic Instruments for Environmental Management and Sustainable Development: Report of the Meeting,* August 1994. Environmental Economics Series, Paper No. 12.

UNEP. *Enhancing Synergies and Mutual Supportiveness of Multilateral Environmental Agreements and the World Trade Organization: A Synthesis Report,* 2001.

UNEP. *Economic Reforms, Trade Liberalization and the Environment: A Synthesis of UNEP Country Projects,* New York and Geneva, 2001.

UNEP. *Fishery Subsidies and Overfishing: Towards a Structured Discussion,* Fisheries and the Environment Series 1, UNEP, 2002

UNEP. *Fishery Subsidies and Marine Resource Management: Lessons Learned from Studies in Argentina and Senegal,* Fisheries and the Environment Series 2, UNEP, 2002

UNEP. *Energy Subsidies: Lessons Learned in Assessing their Impact and Designing Policy Reforms,* UNEP, Geneva, 2003.

UNEP, *Economic Instruments in Biodiversity-Related MEAs,* UNEP, Geneva, 2004.

US Energy Information Administration. "Impacts of a 10-Percent Renewable Portfolio Standard," February 2002.

Wallis, Paul. "Transferable Fishing Quotas: Experience in OECD Countries," in *Implementing Domestic Tradable Permits for Environmental Protection: Proceedings,* OECD, Paris, 2000.

Wiser, Ryan. "State RPS Policies: the Good, the Bad, and the Ugly." NARUC Winter Meetings, Washington, DC, 25 February 2003.

Annex A : A Primer on Economic Instruments

This Annex provides a brief overview of the structure and application of common EIs. As outlined in the text, the instruments are usually implemented to achieve one of a handful of objectives: establishing property rights, recovering revenues, ensuring fair returns on asset sales, protecting against environmental damages from activities, or subsidizing the transition to cleaner alternatives. The sections below provide more detail on each area, including how the policy instruments work and what parameters can be altered in order to modify the policy impact.

One perhaps obvious, but nonetheless important caveat, is that these descriptions are generalizations of policy approaches. Where social, political, or economic pressures on people are severe (e.g., populations facing starvation or corrupt regimes seeking to sell national assets), environmentally-detrimental behaviour is likely to dominate regardless of what policy constraint is supposedly in place. However, under a range of more normal conditions, EIs can be extremely effective tools.

1) Establishing property rights; clarifying or improving existing ones.

A range of instruments including permits, quotas, licensing or concessions, and litigation rights aim to achieve this policy objective. Owners tend to take more care to protect their resources than do users who have no stake in the long-term productivity of the resource. Owners are also more willing to invest money to improve these assets, believing they will achieve higher long-term returns, and can use these assets as collateral for loans with which to finance resource management or upgrades. With a well-functioning legal system, clear property rights also empower owners to enforce contracts against vendors or subcontractors who have not properly protected resources during extraction activities. Owners are not necessarily sole individuals: community or corporate ownership is also included.

An important limitation of property-rights is that they work less well when the property is less tangible (e.g., air pollution versus grazing rights) or more widely dispersed (e.g., local air emissions versus global emissions). In addition, market allocations may sometimes need to be constrained by governments to protect the resource base or to avoid "hot spots" where trades concentrate emissions within sub-populations or ecosystems.

a) **Variations:** Depending on how property rights are assigned, allocated, and transferred, owners will face very different incentives, and governments can experience very different costs.

i) *Initial allocation.* Rights can be *given for free* or *auctioned;* auctions raise revenues for governments and provide better price signals. Give-aways are sometimes justified on the ground that they reduce the economic shock to existing producers who previously paid nothing. They may also help overcome political resistance to the new policy. The grants may be based on current (or partial historical) gross emissions *(grandfathering)* or on emissions per unit output *(output based).* Regardless of the method, such grants, by definition, favour the status quo and can create barriers to entry for newer, cleaner firms. *Benchmarking* firms, which is to award permits based on some form of a performance standard, can reduce this bias somewhat, but requires a fair degree of additional administration. If resale markets are not liquid, initial recipients may not face accurate price signals about the value of their resource/pollution rights, under-investing in controls. Often, the aggregate rights available are *capped* at a particular level to protect the resource, a common example of mixing CAC with EI approaches.

ii) *Ownership.* Rights can be owned by individuals, firms, or communally. Communal rights can be a good solution for subsistence communities, though care must be paid to how the community itself sub-allocates these rights to its members and controls new members from entering the community and putting the resource base under excessive pressure again. Where subsistence groups rely on a low level of resource access, a market divided into two branches may be set up with large firms competing for marketable rights and subsistence farmers/ranchers/fishermen granted subsistence access for free.

iii) *Resale.* Rights can be tradable or not. Tradable rights provide better price signals and stronger incentives for improvement, since firms can always earn money if they can reduce their need for the rights via internal reform or innovation. One drawback to marketable rights is that they may marginalize small producers as existing owners sell out to large companies with economies of scale. Even where not marketable to third parties, policies may allow *averaging* of emissions across a plant or company, a process that can also generate substantial efficiencies for industry.

iv) Duration. Rights can be in perpetuity *(ownership rights)* or for a limited period of time *(use rights). Development rights,* such as patents and prospecting rights, can last for a decade or more, but are not permanent. Some permit regimes have rights *expire* to provide increased pressure for innovation on the rights holder. Phased expirations also ensure that there is an active market in the rights as expiring allocations must be repurchased. This helps create a more liquid market for the permits, and more accurate pricing. Longer durations are generally more valuable to the owner, but provide less flexibility to the public to modify the terms by which public resources are used.

v) *Temporal flexibility.* Rights can sometimes be used over multiple years, rather than being restricted to a single year. By allowing firms to avoid premature removal of capital, to average emissions across production cycles, or to ensure adequate time to vet new technologies, temporal flexibility can bring down the cost of achieving a particular environmental goal. *Banking* involves receiving credit for going below the firm's annual allotment in early years, then using or selling credits above its allotment in later years. *Borrowing* is the reverse, where emissions or extraction is higher than allowed in early years, but lower in future years.

b) **Examples:**

i) Market creation: rights are created where previously behaviour was unconstrained. EI-based approaches often allow countries to meet the same pollution target they could stipulate by regulation, but at a lower cost.

(1) Tradable emission/effluent permits

(2) Tradable catch quotas

(3) Tradable development quotas or rights (location stays the same, developer changes)

(4) Transferable development rights (location shifted to less environmentally sensitive area; developer can stay the same or change).

(5) Tradable water shares

(6) Tradable resource shares

(7) Tradable land permits

(8) Tradable offsets/credits

ii) Clarification of basic property rights. Government policies fix existing problems in the ownership of resource rights. Clear title clears the way for longer-term investment and management.

(1) Ownership rights: land titles, water rights, mining rights

(2) Use rights: licensing, fishery access, use concessions

(3) Development rights: patents, prospecting rights

iii) Property rights protection. Government policies make it easier for existing owners to enforce their rights against potential usurpers.

(1) Contract law; right to sue if contracts not followed.

2) Revenue recovery on the provision of public goods and services.

Governments around the world provide wide-ranging goods and services with both direct and indirect environmental impacts. Examples include electricity, water, wastewater treatment, rubbish removal and recycling, hazardous waste collection and treatment, and wide ranging transportation services. When these services are provided free or at subsidized rates the providing agency may be starved for revenue and unable to maintain, upgrade, or expand its infrastructure and service area. In practice, this often means that the poorest or most rural areas get much-delayed access to basic resources, or no access at all. On the demand side, consumers have little incentive to use the resources wisely, generating a corrosive spiral of unchecked over consumption (and sometimes depletion) followed by demands for larger infrastructure, and sometimes by irrational expansion of this infrastructure.

a) **Variations:**

i) *Rate structures* are commonly adjusted so that the poor receive inexpensive (or free) access to a subsistence quantity of the resource (water, energy). *Increasing block rate* structures accomplish this same goal by providing the first units of consumption to all customers inexpensively, then increasing the unit cost substantially for higher usage rates. Special higher rates are often applied to customers (e.g., industries) that require more expensive and specialized services, such as when they discharge more difficult to treat industrial wastewater to a publicly owned wastewater treatment plant.

ii) *Cross subsidies.* Reduced rates are one form of cross-subsidies. As noted above, these can sometimes be used to provide basic services to the poor. Often, however, cross-subsidies also provide below-market prices to heavy industrial users of municipal services, such as aluminum smelters or steel mills. Removing these types of cross-subsidies can improve pricing accuracy and encourage more environmentally-sustainable consumption.

iii) *Recovery rate.* Depending on the political circumstances, revenue requirements can include recovery of public sector administrative overhead, and a fair cost of capital/rate of return on invested public funds. Full recovery of these costs should always be the goal, as doing so provides pricing more in line with the actual cost of tied-up public funds and allow better choices to be made with regards to future investment into substitutes. One caveat: where the public has already built and paid for the infrastructure, encouraging lots of users (of, for example the sewers) to stop using the system can rob a municipality of important revenues if there are easy and cheap ways for these users to cut back. Each situation should be evaluated separately, though full costing should always be used when evaluating new investment.

iv) *Phase-in.* Where users have not historically paid anything for the public services provided, rates may be phased in over a period of time to reduce the transitional hardships. A phased approach can also help avoid the loss of baseline users (as stated above) when the exact cost they can exit the system is not known.

b) **Examples:**
  i) Charges for services provided directly to consumer
      (1) User fees for municipal water, wastewater treatment, energy.
      (2) Collection charges for solid waste pickup.
      (3) Tolls on public roads.
      (4) Access fees (e.g., for recreational access).
  ii) Charges for impacts new demand will put on existing infrastructure
      (1) Impact fees.
  iii) Charges to recover the public sector overhead associated with providing goods and services to users
      (1) Administrative charges.
      (2) Regulatory oversight charges.
      (3) Enforcement action surcharges.

3) Ensuring fair market value is received when selling publicly owned natural resource assets.

Item 2 above addresses operating municipally-owned organizations. In contrast, this class of instruments deals with ways to realize fair market value for public citizens on the sale of municipally-owned infrastructure and organizations (privatization), or on the sale of publicly owned natural resources. Natural resource sales occur on a regular basis in most countries, as the government often owns the land from which the minerals are extracted. Organizational sales occur less frequently, but can be used to allow governments to focus on more basic services, or to bring a fiscal discipline to the enterprise that was politically or organizationally impossible for the government to establish itself. The sums of money involved often run into the billions of dollars; as a result, policy instruments must ensure that this value is not stolen or mismanaged by public officials and their relations.

Transparency is of extreme importance in these situations, and corruption has been endemic throughout the world both with privatizations and with resource concessions. Payment terms need to be clear, and formal procedures for collecting, investing, and safeguarding resultant funds are needed.

Since asset sales are in many ways a windfall, some governments have set up financial management structures to convert the windfall into a more diversified basket of income-producing assets (often stocks and bonds) for the long-term benefit of its citizens. This helps ensure that at least part of the wealth created is protected from short-term political pressures to spend the funds is less productive ways.

a) **Variations:**
  i) *Auction method.* There are a variety of different auction techniques, depending on what type of resource is being sold, and whether there is only one auction winner or multiple ones.
  ii) *Eligible bidders.* Generally, the more bidders, the more competitive the auctions. Opening bidding to international firms, and to groups (e.g., environmental NGOs) who might retire rather than exploit the rights, can increase the returns to the taxpayer. However, countries need to be sure they can take effective enforcement actions against multinationals if there is a problem with how they extract the resources; and are willing to enforce purchases that close off the resource to all extraction.

iii) *Payment structure.* Depending on the certainty of asset value and the goals of the government, sales can have different mixes between cash bonus payments (paid at the time a license is awarded), rental payments (for the right to hold access to resources within a particular year), and contingent payments such as royalties (paid only as resources are extracted and/or sold).

b) **Examples:**
    i) For achieving break-even revenues and/or fair market value on asset sales:
        (1) Competitive auctions for resource rights or access.
        (2) Full privatization of stand-alone enterprises (so long as the bidding process is open and competitive). Where competitive markets exist, pricing structures generally need to rise to cover costs in order for the enterprise to remain viable.
        (3) Partial privatization of stand-alone enterprises through initial public offerings of stock, and the associated adoption of required oversight and accounting procedures. These approaches can often achieve much of the benefit of full privatization; the key issue is whether the remaining government involvement is hands-off, allowing economics to drive decisions, rather than political.
        (4) Institute payment of natural resource royalties.
        (5) Institute payment of excise taxes on natural resource removal.
    ii) For converting windfalls into long-term sustainable wealth:
        (1) Establishment of carefully controlled and independent trust fund to receive some portion of windfall gains. These funds have conservative investment criteria for investment portfolio and diversification, independent governance, transparent financial records, and high barriers for modifying these protections by elected officials.

4) Environmental externalities/financial assurance.

Many industrial and extractive activities cause pollution or other resource damage. A set of economic instruments aims to accomplish three objectives: force the environmental costs into current prices; set up financial mechanisms that protect the public from cleanup costs should the original firm/government fail to do so; and to provide a legal mechanism to sue firms or governments retroactively for the damage their activities have caused. Informational regimes (e.g., mandatory emissions reporting) leverage market forces by exposing below-par performance to customers and neighbours, and by establishing a record of past performance that can support legal action should there be violations.

  a) **Variations:**
    i) *Time:* some EIs spur reductions in the environmental risks associated with current activities; others attempt to recover costs of past damages; and still others help mitigate future environmental risks.
    ii) *Phase-in.* As with most EIs, instruments can be phased in over time to reduce the transitional dislocations.
    iii) *Polluter pays principle.* There are degrees to how closely the entity paying is the one who polluted. It can be the firm, the industry, the region, or all taxpayers. The closer the payments are to the ones causing the problem, the better the price signals will be.
    iv) *Degree of risk control.* Protection against future risks is often done through insurance. Governments can make this tool more effective by allowing only financially strong insurers into the market, and by instituting reinsurance requirements where appropriate. Reinsurers absorb a portion of the potential risks associated with a policy, establishing increased diversification for the insurance market. However, they too must be monitored for financial solvency.

v) *Border adjustments.* Surcharges can be added to competing products coming into the country to offset any competitive disadvantage due to environmental regulation.

b) **Examples:**
    i) Addressing risks of current activities:
        (1) Pollution taxes/permits
    ii) Recovering damages associated with past activities:
        (1) Civil and criminal penalties for natural resource damages.
    iii) Addressing risks of future activities:
        (1) Required liability or environmental insurance
        (2) Performance bonds for proper site remediation/closure. Bonds can be issued for environmental performance, land reclamation bonds, waste delivery bonds, environmental accident bonds, forest management bonds.
        (3) Deposit/refund systems for proper product returns

5) Subsidizing transition to cleaner alternatives.

New technologies or alternative resource management practices may have demonstrated environmental benefits relative to current practice. EIs that subsidize these alternatives can benefit environmental quality by accelerating a market shift to these preferable approaches. Once subsidies are available, however, many groups will seek to obtain them; not all will be justified. Care and attention are needed to ensure that the subsidies flow narrowly to the desired recipients if the original objectives of the policies are to be achieved.

a) **Variations:**
    i) *Point of support.* Subsidies can support activities linked to desired practices (research into wind power), or they can be paid only when the desired practices are actually applied in the market place (tax credit for each delivered kWh of wind power). Rewarding only successful innovation is generally much more cost efficient and productive, and much of the development and marketing risk remains in the private sector.
    ii) *Magnitude of support.* Subsidy levels can range from 100 per cent (grants) to much smaller levels associated with EIs such as revolving funds (small interest rate subsidies). Efficiently providing only what is needed to make a technology economic, but no more, allows limited public funds to have a much greater impact. Renewable Energy Portfolio standards, for example, force clean energy providers to compete against each other for the minimum level of subsidy at which they can provide clean energy. This type of an approach helps make subsidies both more efficient and more dynamic over time.

b) **Examples:**
    i) Grant-based subsidies: soft loans, direct funding, provision of hard currency at below market rates.
    ii) Financing-based subsidies: Soft loans, revolving funds, sectoral funds, green funds, public interest rate subsidies or loan guarantees.
    iii) Tax-based subsidies: tax credits, tax breaks, tax exemptions, tax differentiation, accelerated write-offs.
    iv) Risk-based subsidies: subsidized insurance or reinsurance, liability caps, public sector indemnification.

Annex B: Global Metrics of Environmental and Government Performance

Local policy makers face a sensitive political situation when trying to judge and assess -- even qualitatively -- the capabilities and levels of corruption in the institutions of which they are a part, or with whom they must work. A number of efforts are currently underway to develop indices and cross-country rankings for these sensitive measures. These indices do entail judgments and approximations, and none are perfect, nevertheless they do provide an important outside source both to help assess domestic conditions and to justify evaluations that civil servants make. This Annex presents a number of the more promising metrics, but is not an exhaustive listing.

Environmental Sustainability Index

The Environmental Sustainability Index (ESI) is an initiative of the Global Leaders of Tomorrow Task Force of the World Economic Forum. The index measures overall progress towards environmental sustainability for 142 countries. There are five core components evaluated: environmental systems, reducing stresses, reducing human vulnerability, social and institutional capacity, and global stewardship. There are 68 underlying variables which combine measures "of current conditions, pressures on those conditions, human impacts, and social responses".

Source: Global Leaders of Tomorrow Environment Task Force, 2002 *Environmental Sustainability Index,* 2002. Available at:
http://www.ciesin.columbia.edu/indicators/ESI.

Corruption Perceptions Index

The Corruption Perceptions Index (CPI) is compiled by Transparency International. It is a "poll of polls", drawing on 14 surveys from seven institutions regarding perceptions about corruption levels in the government. Polled individuals include business people, academics, and country analysts. Only countries with at least three surveys are included, which means some high-corruption nations are left off the listing.

Source: Transparency International Press Release, "Corrupt political elites and unscrupulous investors kill sustainable growth in its tracks, highlights new index," Berlin, 28 August 2002. Data available at:
http://www.transparency.org/pressreleases_archive/2002/2002.08.28.cpi.en.html

World Bank Efforts

The World Bank has been working on aggregate governance indices since 1997. Using 194 data measures from 17 data sources compiled by 15 separate organizations, the Bank integrates them into six aggregate index areas. Rule of Law is used as a proxy for the baseline legal institutions within a country. Voice and Accountability can serve as a proxy for the strength of the political institutions. The Bank also tracks the work of others and maintains a fairly extensive listing of these ongoing efforts.

Resources: World Bank data sets are available at:
http://www.worldbank.org/wbi/governance/wp-governance.htm.

Additional resource: Daniel Kaufman, Aart Kraay, and Pablo Zoido-Lobaton, Governance Matters II: *Updated Indicators for 2000/2001,* World Bank Policy Research Working Paper 2772, February 2002.

Annex C: Detailed Analysis of Case Study Applications of Economic Instruments

Title	ITQs for fisheries resources in South Africa
Country	South Africa
Problem Definition	
Environmental impacts	Over-fishing leading to increasing decline in fish catches and sustainability of the fisheries. Some shortages evident in the 1960s, as key stocks faced sharp declines. By mid-1970s, declines in hake, pilchards, and anchovy were evident. This was the result of over-fishing by both domestic and international fleets
Social impacts	Fisheries in question comprise 1% of GDP, provide 35,000 direct jobs and 100,000 indirect ones. Fishing rights (as of 1996) were 90% allocated to large commercial companies; black fishing communities had less than 1% of the total allowable catch (TAC).
Solution Implemented	Since 1997, the country has moved towards use of ITQs under the Marine Living Resources Bill of 1997. A portion of the ITQs are withheld to support black-owned businesses and coastal communities, to offset the heavy concentration of fishing rights in white-only businesses that had previously existed. Access control supplements the ITQs: total and seasonal closures protect specific fishery areas; strict monitoring of 200 mile exclusion zones prevents poaching of stocks by foreign vessels.
Summary Analysis	
Efficacy of existing policy at solving problem	There is no detailed assessment of the success of the ITQ yet. Quota revenues, rather than being used to support resource management, are directed to the general treasury. There is a small levy that goes to the Seas Fisheries Fund to support research. The approach does seem to increased market share for domestic fleets relative to foreign, and to small communities and black-owned businesses, relative to white-only businesses. Although ITQs improve the efficiency of TAC allocation, intense political pressure to increase the TACs themselves remain. This pressure has also been exhibited through efforts to reduce the monitoring and enforcement capability of the country, critical programme elements if the ITQs are to be effective. Evidence suggests that illegal fishing by those without a quota remains a problem.
Rationale for success/failure	+Strong success models from adoption of ITQs in other countries greatly increased likelihood of implementation. -Inadequate monitoring and enforcement risks all potential gains from the ITQ approach. -Diversion of quota revenues to the general Treasury weakens the ability of the Environment Ministry to build a strong program. +However, transfer of authority to the Environment Ministry from the Industry Ministry in the early 1980s helped shift the overall policy focus from resource extraction to resource management.
Unanswered questions	-Is there a strong technical basis for setting quota limits today? -Has there been an increase in the mutual monitoring of fleets by permit holders?
Institutional Baseline Conditions in Country	
Legal	
Fiscal	
Government institutions	2001 Corruption Perceptions Index (38 of 91)

Environmental	2002 ESI: 48.7 (rank 77 of 142) Relevant component rankings: Environmental Governance (33 of 142); Reducing Ecosystem Stress (47 of 142); Environmental Systems (91 of 142)
Detail on Policy Process	
History of response	Early control efforts focused on reducing access to fisheries by implementation of a 200 nautical mile fishing zone to keep out foreign fleets and increasing the minimum required mesh size in nets to reduce depletion of immature fish. Catch limits, in the form of a Total Allowable Catch, was set for at least some fish species (e.g., hake) beginning in the late 1970s. This was supplemented by efforts to reduce the number of vessels and the closure of critical areas (mainly where pelagic fish are targeted). Exclusion of foreign commercial vessels was implemented in 1983, along with a conservative management strategy. Research has also been conducted to identify the benefits of long-lining rather than netting on the overall health of the hake fishery.
	Quotas to allocate the TAC were set initially set by the Minister of Economic Affairs, Industries, and Agriculture, upon advice from officials in the capital. In 1983, general management of the Sea Fisheries Act was transferred to the Minstry of Environment Affairs. Criticisms of the Minister-allocated quota system led to a transfer of quota setting authority to a statutory board in 1986, a more formal Quota Board in 1988 (which became effective only in 1990). During the 1990s, political considerations led to efforts to increase the quotas flowing to black communities and companies. Foreign-owned vessels still have very limited access to key fisheries. Since 1997, reliance on the market to allocate TACs, through the ITQs, has grown.
Evaluation of past success/failure	CAC approaches did contribute to some recovery of catch rates, such as in the core hake fishery.
Rationale for using EI	Fishery depletion remained a concern, and created a strong need for information to support a more scientific basis for fisheries and catch management. ITQs would provide a more flexible and less biased mechanism to allocate TAC than would the Quota boards, and provide individual fishermen with a more direct stake in effective long term fisheries management.
Legal basis for EI	Basic involvement in fisheries management originates with the Sea Fisheries Act of 1940, plus superceding Acts in 1973 and 1988. Direct authority for the use of ITQs comes under the Marine Living Resources Bill of 1997.
Stakeholder involvement	Extensive public consultations, including much education on the application of ITQs in other parts of the world. Local communities, scientists, and other resource users are organized and actively involved in the management of ocean resources.
Lead agencies	Ministry of Environment Affairs
Key barriers addressed	
Detail on Policy Response	
Allocation of initial rights	Information reviewed suggested that ITQs were initially allocated for free, and somewhat arbitrarily.
On-going monitoring process	Appears to be weak and under-funded. Influenced by political lobbying to increase overall TAC and to reduce the capability of the State to curb illegal fishing.
Current successes	
Remaining gaps/risks	Proposed reforms attempt to replace giving away fishing rights with auctions, and earmarking fees/royalties from these rights back to the fishery oversight function.
Source(s)	Summarized by Herminia Franscisco based on Jaap Arntzen. 1999. *Economic Instruments and the Southern African Environment: Synthesis of Experiences of Five SADC Countries.*

Title	**Grassland pricing reform, Philippines**
Country	Philippines
Problem Definition	
Environmental impacts	Ranchers are provided with 25 year Pasture Lease Agreements (PLA), renewable for another 25 years, at very low grazing fees (approximately US$ 0.30/hectare/year). As a result, a relatively small group of people has gained control over much of the public grasslands for the 50-year leases. The ability to shift cattle to new pastures they control has also reduced the incentive for sound management of the pastureland, and led to resource degradation in many parts of the country.
Social impacts	Policies seem likely to result in over-concentration in access to grazing rights. However, they probably do encourage human settlement in some more remote, less hospitable areas.
Solution Implemented	Existing grazing fees were increased from PhP15 per hectare/year to PhP200/ha/yr. Original efforts to have higher fees on better land classes were shelved. While more than 10 times higher than the prior charge, the rates are still believed to be only slightly more than half the lowest economically-justifiable rent on the land. In addition, the charge had a five-year phase-in period. To support the transition, the policy included increased technical assistance as well as fee reductions for sound land management.
Summary Analysis	
Efficacy of existing policy at solving problem	Although there is clear agreement that more accurate pricing, coupled with enforcement of operating and management plans, would greatly improve both access to and management of public grasslands, political reality has precluded this solution. As a result, ranchers continue to have low cost, long-term access to public grazing lands with little incentive for proper land management. DENR continues to have poor ability to enforce management standards. ERDB has increased responsibilities for technical outreach, but no effective plan on how to do so yet. To obtain reduced grazing fees associated with sound land management, ranchers must initiate review by DENR for and have pasture management plans approved. With cost savings so large, there is a potential of corruption that is of concern. A number of ranchers have refused to pay the higher fee. As a result, DENR ends up collecting nothing from them and has little capability to carry out full enforcement. Furthermore, during a trip to the region in early 2002, a top government official promised to reduce the fee substantially (to PhP40 from PhP200) "to encourage breeding and create 60,000 jobs" (Luzon Bulletin, 1/6/02). This statement undermined current efforts to collect the higher fees, and led DENR to suspend its collection pending formal clarification on how to proceed. Personnel pointed out that decades of grazing fees at 15 PhP did not spur investment in the cattle industry, so were not clear on how one could conclude that PhP 40 would do so.
Rationale for success/failure	Fees remain too low, and politically difficult to adjust. Ranching interests remain extremely strong and oppose any shifts to more market-oriented rates. Groups who may be negatively affected by the current leasing arrangements do not seem mobilized. -Fees that are collected are remitted to the Treasury rather than retained to support the land management program. -Lease terms remain very long and holding costs very low, allowing high concentration of access to pasturelands to continue. -Political resistance prevented the use of market auctions to allocate grazing rights, an approach that could have removed the government from the role of having to set grazing rates. -While DENR has sometimes revoked leases, this has normally been done due to abandonment or use for non-grazing purposes. There is little evidence of revocation due to improper or destructive grazing practices.
Unanswered questions	

Institutional Baseline Conditions in Country	
Legal	
Fiscal	The Philippines already has an infrastructure in place for collecting fees from ranchers.
Government institutions	
Environmental	DENR has lacked resources to oversee management plans. Internationally-funded efforts going back to 1990 have attempted to build capacity within DENR related to natural resource accounting, technical standards, and grasslands pricing reforms.

Detail on Policy Process	
History of response	PLAs have been used since the 1950s. Fees were first imposed in 1961 at an average rate of less than US $0.01/hectare per year. Fees were not increased until 20 years later, reaching only US $0.02/hectare per year; then again in 1991 to the current rate of US $0.30. Compliance with the fees has generally been quite high, which is not surprising given the very low rate. To exert some control over grazing processes, the Department of Environment and Natural Resources (DENR) requires annual operating plans, and a management plan every eighth year. However, there is virtually no follow-up monitoring to ensure plans are actually being implemented. This is the result of insufficient funding as well as difficult terrain to oversee. There is common recognition that fees are too low. To address the problem, DENR's Ecosystems Research Development Board evaluated what the true economic rent should be, the cost of various measures to rehabilitate existing damages, and the economics of alternative land uses. They did not evaluate options for auctioning, rather than giving, grazing rights to the ranchers. The economic rents were determined to be far higher than the current levels, though the ERDB proposed allowing 80% of the incremental payment be used to fix damage on the existing grasslands.
Evaluation of past success/failure	Past efforts to charge for access and to ensure appropriate land management on existing leases have been plagued by the exact same problems that have prevented the most recent effort from obtaining more reasonable lease rates.
Rationale for using EI	EIs, through user fees, have been in effect for nearly 50 years. While collection levels were high, fee rates were far too low to cover either programme costs or provide proper incentives for sound land management. Fee reforms were chosen over lease auctions due to political resistance.
Legal basis for EI	Original basis for grazing fees was through Administrative Order 08 in 1961. The initial fee increase was authorized in the Forest Land Grazing Lease Agreement of 1982. The most current fee adjustment was authorized by Department Administrative Order 2001-05, which took effect in August 2001.
Stakeholder involvement	There have been a series of public hearings run by ERDB to discuss existing and proposed grazing fees. Ranchers were already well organized as a stakeholder group, and strongly opposed rate increases. They argued that the government should view their presence on the land as a benefit in that it curbed squatting by migrants. They also mobilized strong political actions against the ERDB and DENR to oppose the rate increases.
Lead agencies	Ecosystems Research Development Board (ERDB) and the Department of Environment and Natural Resources.
Key barriers addressed	Key barriers have not successfully been addressed: existing damage is not being addressed by the current policy, nor are grazing rights at levels that would encourage more appropriate resource use.

Detail on Policy Response	
Allocation of initial rights	There has been no effort to auction grazing rights. Rights have continued with existing holders, with the price of those rights (through an annual rental fee) set by statute. The price of the rights does not adjust automatically for inflation, and is far below appropriate market levels. Government assessments suggest grazing rights should be divided into three classes, with annual rentals ranging from PhP358 to PhP542, between 24 and 36 times the current levels.
On-going monitoring process	DENR has not been able to generate an effective monitoring and enforcement process.
Current successes	Grazing fees have risen somewhat, but still remain far below market. Public research efforts have yielded useful results on economic fee rates and costs to recover damaged lands.
Remaining gaps/risks	There has been strong political resistance to market-based grazing fees. Current rates are not set in a dynamic, market-oriented way, and remain very much subject to political pressures. The regulating agency has not been able to supplement its fiscal policies with credible monitoring oversight to prevent land degradation.
Source(s)	Case study compiled by Herminia Franciso. Additional sources include: Personal Communication with Luzon Bulletin, 6 January 2002.

Title	Water charge for river basin access, Brazil
Country	Brazil
Problem Definition	
Environmental impacts	Increasing degradation in many Brazilian rivers led to a desire for action to protect them. The rivers cross both state and international borders, so solutions required a coordinated response across many government agencies. In addition, there were hundreds of affected users who must be brought into any environmental management system that is created.
Social impacts	Impacts vary by river basin. In some, there are many small industrial and agricultural users. In addition, municipal users of bulk water form the basis of supply to much of the population.
Solution Implemented	Based on input from empowered River Basin sub-committees, it was decided to implement a system of water user fees, varying depending on the amount used and pollution content of the activity. Political pressure led the charge levels to be based on recovering administrative and monitoring costs only. Over the longer-term, officials hope charges can be increased enough to affect the consumption and pollution patterns of resource users. To date, many River Basins have yet to implement charges, and some that have continue to have rates that provide little incentive to conserve, to curb pollution discharges, or that recover the full costs of associated services and infrastructure.
Summary Analysis	
Efficacy of existing policy at solving problem	Establishing the legal authority to implement charges of any kind has been a very long process. Federal involvement seemed necessary to address the complex issues of multiple and overlapping jurisdictional interests prevalent in Brazil. This finding matches that in other countries. (Dourojeanni, 2001 p.33). Despite the long gestation period to establish a legal framework for water charges, problems remain. Charge implementation remains slow, and fees that have been implemented appear too low, and are sometimes voluntary. None of these attributes are likely to address the core problems driving river basin degradation. Furthermore, there is not enough information on proposed feed structures to evaluate whether there are substantial cross-subsidies in the rate design. Industry groups, for example, have expressed concerned that households and farms will be exempt from the charges, putting all the burden on them.
Rationale for success/failure	-Greater involvement of affected groups early-on, as well as more technical analysis of the likely benefits of charges on water quantity and quality, would both of have helped achieve a positive result much sooner. -Earlier federal involvement in establishing the legal frameworks might have been helpful, as would more rigorous deadlines for establishing operational and self-supporting River Basin Committees. Dourojeanni, (p. 35) suggests that the initial scope of activities needs to be moderate, but expand over time. -Although charge systems have been promoted, establishing guidelines on how to measure the costs of services provided by the Committees. In addition, technical support to improve the ability of the Committees to monitor water usage would help ensure fees are adequate, flexible, and equitable to various user groups.
Unanswered questions	-What are the main barriers to fee implementation in the Basins that have not yet done so? -What types of cross-subsidies remain in fees that do exist, and how will they affect efforts to conserve water and reduce pollution? -To what degree have sub-basin committees been organized? -How successful have the Basin Committees (or Water Agencies) been at accurately measuring consumption and collecting fees?
Institutional Baseline Conditions in Country	
Legal	Unknown
Fiscal	Unknown
Government institutions	Brazil has a fairly effective set of government institutions at the municipal, state, and federal levels. It is not clear that the newly formed River Basin Committees have adequate political strength or technical capacity to set and enforce water user fees.

Environmental	Unknown
Detail on Policy Process	
History of response	Efforts to improve river management date back at least to 1978, when the Committee on Joint Studies on River Basins was set up (Seroa da Motta and Reis, 1994, p. 21). Separate committees were set up at some of the most problematic river basins in Brazil, and comprised users, polluters, and government agencies. The committees had no power to regulate, enforce, or tax: therefore, most of the relevant committees' proposals were not implemented, and even involvement with the committees by stakeholders was fairly weak. (Huber et al., 1998, p.32).
	The Irrigation Law of 1979 (Law No. 6,662) set up rules for use of public waters for irrigation. It set up minimum river discharges for all seasons (permanent waters), with the surplus available for diversion (eventual waters). It also established the basis for charging for use, with rates for use of eventual waters set equal to half the rate for permanent waters. Availability of the eventual waters was intermittent, while that of permanent waters was assumed at 100%. (Campos and Studart, 2000, p. 150).
	It took an amendment to the Brazilian constitution in 1988, enacted in the face of severe river degradation, to finally introduce the power for the basin committees to tax and regulate. This legislative reform also made firms liable for environmental damages and allowed actions to be taken against managers (Seroa da Motta and Reis, p. 13). Legislative action to reformulate these committees followed. Conflicts arose on the relative power of different levels of government, whether taxes would be earmarked for usage on river basin protection, and whether charge levels should cover basin management costs only, or environmental damages as well. Progress has been slow.
	In 1989, an attempt was made to establish a National System of Water Resource Management. In 1993, a much reformulated proposal was resubmitted to Congress. This legislation, based on the French model of water management, proposed a series of water charges based on quality and quantity. This included fees both on use and discharge. The system is to be secured by 6% of operational fees that are contributed by hydroelectric companies.
	The Federal Water Law, passed in January 1997, created a legate framework for managing water resources. The Law recognizes water as an economic good, and allows river basin management councils to charge for water. Fees have three purposes: to make the public see water as an economic (rather than a free good); to encourage rationale use of the resource; and to finance Basin Water Management Plans. Currently, the few Basins that are charging fees do so only to finance Management Plans; fees are too low to ration use. (Campos and Studart, 2000, p. 151).
	Overall, the preparation of the Framework Water Law, as well as subsequent regulations, took approximately 10 years. (Sarmento, 2003). Water charges are now in place in the Paraiba do Sul basin, and in Ceara state. An additional ten basins will implement charges by 2008. (ibid.).
Evaluation of past success/failure	The River Basin committee formulated management plans, but had neither the general mandate nor the financial resources to be able to implement its plans. Analysts also expressed concern that the committees did not adequately integrate public good aspects of water basin investment projects or the impact of transboundary pollutants entering from tributary rivers. (Seroa da Motta and Reis, 1994.)
	Campos and Studart point to different water-related conditions prevailing in different parts of Brazil. One is characterized by abundant water and little polluting activity, such as the Amazon. In these regions, the authors argue water charges are unlikely to take hold. A second group includes abundant water, but also lots of polluting activity. In these regions, charges are under discussion or near implementation. The third region includes scarce water with some pollution activity that further increases the pressure on water resources. The state of Ceara is on example, and was an early adapter of water charges, having had some form of charge for most of the 20th century. However, fees were often set low and quickly eroded by high inflation. At some points the cost of collecting the fee exceeded the revenues raised. (Campos and Studart, 2000, p. 151). Since 1975, a more formal charge system has been implemented under the delegated authority of COGERH (Company of Water Management of the State) and covers municipal, industrial, and agricultural uses. However, rates are set by statute rather than market based. Agricultural tariffs cover only operation and maintenance on the distribution system, not the cost of water or capital costs of the irrigation systems. There are other problems. In the commercial sector, the government has used water discounts of 50% as a fiscal incentives to selected industries. In the agricultural sector, bills "are charged to a whole project, divided equally among irrigators". As a result, there is little incentive to conserve. (ibid. p. 152).

Rationale for using EI	Despite the existence of the River Basin Committee, it became clear that the Committee did not have sufficient authority to actually address the problem of river degradation. In the 1988 Constitution, the mandate of the Committee was broadened, and each basin committee formulated a recovery plan. Most of the plans involved introducing water charges based on the use and pollution content of the activities. Although the original objective was to set fees for both recovering costs of basin management and to encourage conservation, actual fee levels to date generally do only the former.
Legal basis for EI	The legal basis for the charges has evolved somewhat piece-meal. States with heightened concerns over water quality or scarcity had legal structures in place to regulate and charge for water decades ago. However, the full legal basis for the charges nationally did not arrive until January 1997 with the passage of the Bill on New Water Management System. In addition, some of the early charge systems had fees set so low that they provided neither an incentive to conserve or fees to oversee water management efforts.
Stakeholder involvement	There are indications that one reason national water policies in Brazil did not progress as they should have in part because of the absence of participatory consultations with the various sectors. Despite not being included in official meetings, the industrial water users were very well organized and vocal. In addition, the long gestation period of authorizing legislation, and the relatively slow adoption of charge schemes since the Water Law, all indicate that resistance to charges by those who will pay the most remains strong. Based on a review of Basin authorities in multiple countries (including Brazil) Dourojeanni (p. 35) advocates that users be part of the authorities from the outset, and that they further organize by watercourses and canals to ensure joint planning capabilities at multiple levels. He suggests making registration and participation in such organizations a prerequisite for obtaining any technical support or other services from the Basin Committees.
Lead agencies	The federal government has jurisdiction over water bodies with potential for hydraulic energy, or which cross or border more than one state or another country. The Water Law of 1997 established two federal institutions to help coordinate water management. These are the Water Resource National Council (CNRH) and an executive federal water agency (ANA), both of which are directly linked to the Ministry of the Environment. (Seroa da Motta and Feres, forthcoming). Pollution control is shared between federal, state, and municipal authorities. River Basin Committees can operate in an entire river basin; the river sub-basin of any tributary to the main watercourse; the tributary to that tributary; or a group of contiguous river basins or sub-basins. (Dourojeanni, p. 63). River Basins governing watercourses that are federal property must be established by an Act of the Brazilian president. Basin Committees for each River Basin are comprised of 40% government authorities (federal, state, municipal), 20% civil entities, and 40% users. (Sarmento, 2003). Water Agencies are the administrative arm of the Basin Committees, and serve to register users, collect fees for water use, review and comment on projects to be financed by Basin fees. They also monitor financial management of fees, and arrange and oversee processes such as budget development and technical studies. (Dourojeanni, p. 64).
Key barriers addressed	Legal hurdles to integrated management of River Basins and fee collection from users were resolved through federal legislation. Fee setting and implementation remain problematic.
Detail on Policy Response	
Allocation of initial rights	There appears to have been no new restrictions on use or discharge of water associated with the river basin charge plan. Any user willing to pay could continue as before.
On-going monitoring process	While oversight is delegated primarily to the River Basin Commissions, charges have been implemented in only a few places. One of these, Ceara, demonstrates that the process remains in its early stages of development. Campos and Studart note that "even when water is understood as a well-defined product, it is still not capable of being controlled an measured in the whole State under the current structures". (Campos and Studart, p. 153).
Current successes	After much effort, Brazil has established most of the legal conditions under which basin management can be decentralized and water charges can be implemented. The legal authority has begun a process of rational water management, but this process is still in its infancy.
Remaining gaps/risks	Implementation, rate structure, and monitoring are all major gaps in the current effort that will ultimately determine whether this programme will solve the problem it was intended to solve or not. Resistance to charges for bulk water remain, even in water scarce regions such as Ceara. (ibid. p. 153).

Source(s)	-Ronaldo Seroa de Motta and Eustaquio J. Reis. 1994. *The Application of Economic Instruments in Environmental Policy: The Brazilian Case*
	-Richard Huber, Jack Ruitenbeek, and Ronaldo Seroa de Motta. 1998. *Market-based Instruments for Environmental Policymaking in Latin America and the Carribean: Lessons from Eleven Countries,* World Bank Discussion Paper no. 381.
	-Saremento, Jair. "Multi-Sectoral Approaches in River Basin Management," presented at *Water Week 2003: Water and Development,* World Bank, Washington, DC, 6 June 2003.
	-J.N.B. Campos and T.M.C. Studart. "An Historical Perspective on the Administration of Water in Brazil," *Water International,* V. 25, No. 1, pp. 148-156, March 2000.
	-Axel Dourojeanni. *Water management at the river basin level: challenges in Latin America,* United Nationals, CEPAL, Natural Resources and Infrastructure Division, Santiago, Chile, August, 2001.
	-Ronaldo Seroa da Motta and Feres, "Country Case: Brazil" in: Seroa da Motta, R. *Water Charge Instruments for Environmental Management in Latin America: from Theoretical to Practical Issues,* IDB, Washington, Segundo Dialogo Regional de Política de Medio Ambiente, forthcoming.

Title	**Strengthening user rights for biodiversity conservation and sustainable use: Mankote Mangrove, St Lucia**
Country	St. Lucia
Problem Definition	
Environmental impacts	The Mankote Mangrove comprises the largest contiguous tract of mangrove in St. Lucia, and 20% of the total mangrove area in the country. Widespread and uncontrolled charcoal harvesting from the trees put the mangroves into severe environmental decline. The loss posed a significant threat to the many ecosystem services mangroves provide, including maintaining coastal stability and water quality, serving as a fish breeding and nursery ground, trapping silt, and providing important bird habitat.
Social impacts	Charcoal was harvested by local subsistence populations. These people were extremely poor and had no legal right to any use of the publicly owned mangrove resources. They did not have obvious alternative employment should their access to the mangroves be cut off due to resource depletion or degradation.
Solution Implemented	Subsistence users were organized into an informal cooperative and given communal legal and exclusive rights to harvest the charcoal. They became involved with a joint monitoring programme with a regional NGO, the Caribbean Natural Resources Institute, to obtain accurate and timely information on the overall health of the mangrove resource. Flanking measures to increase the supply of wood outside of the mangrove reserves, and to create alternative job options for charcoal harvesters were also implemented. Tourism has been one important alternative.
Summary Analysis	
Efficacy of existing policy at solving proble	The programme has halted and reversed the decline in the Mankote mangroves. The density and size of trees have both increased. Charcoal harvests have been more or less maintained, and the range of employment options for this population subgroup have increased somewhat.
Rationale for success/failure	-Early tacit approval by government for CANARI to work with the charcoal extractors in an innovative and then-controversial endeavor. -Formal recognition of property rights for subsistence charcoal extractors was a key element in ensuring commitment to, and ability to enforce, sustainable harvest practices. Long delays in this recognition made the effort somewhat less effective than it could have been. -Provision of group tenure, encouraging integrated management of the entire resource base and monitoring of cutting patterns by other members of the cooperative. -Establishment of cooperatives for the extractors, to provide a management unit for organizing and overseeing cutting rights; and formalization of rules of extraction that help protect resource base. -Strong and continuous assessment programme to evaluate overall health of the resource base. -Protections against other threats to mangrove health, such as development, and least for now.
Unanswered questions	-Quality of continued management. -Degree to which development and remains a long-term threat, as well as increased pressure from crabbing and fishing within Mankote. -Are the exclusive cutting rights, granted by a letter from the Deputy Chief Fisheries Officer, supportable should there be legal action at some future date? -Ability of existing members of cooperatives to sell rights to others, and implications of this on long-term viability of the approach.
Institutional Baseline Conditions in Country	
Legal	Widespread self-monitoring of cutting by different members of the cooperative (each protecting their individual interests) has made enforcement of the agreement both easier and less expensive.
Fiscal	
Government institutions	
Environmental	St. Lucia's natural resource management agencies are perpetually under funded. Involvement of CANARI made the change in resource management possible.

Detail on Policy Process	
History of response	St. Lucia's Forest, Soil and Water Conservation Ordinance of 1946 and its Wildlife Production Act of 1980 both gave the government a legal framework for regulating harvesting activities on public lands. However, little was actually done to regulate or control the harvesting of charcoal using mangrove wood.
	In 1986, the area was declared a marine reserve, helping to reduce the risk of the grove being developed.
	Subsistence charcoal producers did implement a number of positive practices on their own. They cut on a rotational basis, allowing time for the trees to regenerate before returning. Species that did not make good charcoal were also left to provide cover and impede evaporation of the swamp.
	Following the formation of ACAPG, the group committed to a set of rules for sustainable use of the mangrove. These included a ban on cutting any trees that lined the waterways, the preservation of large trees, and cutting on a slant to preserve the tree's stump. Cutting rights were also organized, with each charcoal producer getting access to one area for a season, and rotating to a different area the next season. Cutting areas are well known to avoid conflicts between cutters and encourage monitoring of compliance behaviour by other members of the cooperative. However, these rules were not formalized until 1996, when ACAPG was granted exclusive rights to the timber in the Mankote reserve.
Evaluation of past success/failure	Prior to the establishment of ACAPG and institution of joint monitoring of the resource base, there was no effective control at all on charcoal production, leading to widespread degradation of the resource base.
Rationale for using EI	This is a property rights approach that clarifies use rights in the form of charcoal harvesting rights. The approach made sense because the subsistence harvesters were the primary cause of the problem. Yet, with no formal rights to the resource, they had little incentive to invest in longer-term resource management.
Legal basis for EI	Development activity in Mankote was prevented through the 1986 designation of the land as a marine reserve. In 1996, the Department of Fisheries, which oversees the reserve, formalized the long-standing de facto agreement under which ACAPG member got exclusive rights to the use of timber resources from within the grove.
Stakeholder involvement	Extensive involvement with ACAPG, the charcoal producers cooperative.
Lead agencies	Caribbean Natural Resources Institute (CANARI, a regional NGO); Aupicon Charcoal and Agricultural Producers Group (ACAPG), the cooperative of charcoal producers established during this initiative.
Key barriers addressed	
Detail on Policy Response	
Allocation of initial rights	Initial rights were given for free to members of ACAPG, the charcoal harvesters cooperative. They are subsistence harvesters, and securing their tenure increased their interest in sustainable management of the resource. It is not clear from available sources how these rights are transferred among parties.
On-going monitoring process	Regular monitoring of the mangrove resource remains an important activity. We have no information on how frequently it is being done, or who pays for it.
Current successes	By most metrics, including forest health, diversification of job base, and earnings of subsistence population, the policy response has been successful.
Remaining gaps/risks	Mankote and surrounding land remains a target for large-scale development, especially for resort and golf courses. Continued vigilance is needed to protect the mangrove from these threats.
	Efforts to shift from mangrove to hardwood from plantations near Mankote have had limited success. This is in part due to the lack of experience the producers have with agriculture and marketing.

Source(s)	Case material compiled by Markus Lehmann based on the following sources:
	De Beauville-Scott, S. 2000: *A preliminary assessment of the basin of the Mankote Mangrove, Saint Lucia, West Indies.* Natural Resource Management Programme. Department of Natural Resource Management. Faculty of Science and Technology, Cave Hill, Barbados. *(mimeo)*
	Geoghegan, T. and A. H. Smith. 1998: *Conservation and sustainable Livelihoods: Collaborative Management of the Mankote Mangrove, St. Lucia.* Community Participation in Forest Management. CANARI.
	Portecop, J. and E. Benito-Espinal. 1985: *The mangroves of St. Lucia; a preliminary survey.* CANARI technical Report no. 45.
	Smith, A. H. and F. Berkes. 1993: "Community-based use of mangrove resources in St. Lucia". *Intern. J. Environmental Studies,* vol. 43, pp. 123-131.
	St. Lucia, Ministry of Agriculture, Forestry and Fisheries, the Permanent Secretary 2002: *Incentive Measures. Case Studies and Best Practices on Incentive Measures and Their Implementation.* Submission by the Government of St. Lucia to the Secretariat of the Convention on Biological Diversity. http://www.biodiv.org/programmes/socio-eco/incentives/case-studies.asp.
	World Resource Institute 2000: "Managing Mankote Mangrove". *World Resources Institute 2000-2001. People and Ecosystems. The Fraying Web of Life.* World Resource Institute, Washington D.C., pp.176-177.

Title	**Fishery ITQs in Chile**
Country	Chile
Problem Definition	
Environmental impacts	Fish stocks were increasingly depleted under the increasing privatization of the fishing industry that has occurred since 1973. Increasing fishing pressures especially on the pelagic fisheries drove catches higher, until they peaked in 1986.
Social impacts	Two concerns dominated the initial implementation of ITQs. The first involved artisanal fisherman. The concern was that under an ITQ system, they would be excluded from the market and lose their livelihoods. As a result, they continue to fish without an ITQ system. The second involved competition between northern and southern fishery corporations, with each trying to influence the allocation and bidding structures to their advantages, rather than to the advantage of long-term fisheries management.
Solution Implemented	The regulatory solution has varied depending on the type of fishery. For fisheries with low exploitation and primarily caught by artisanal fishermen (who use small boats and tend to stay close to shore), an open access system remains in effect.
	ITQs have been implemented for standard fisheries, with separate subclasses for fisheries in recovery and emerging fisheries (defined as less than 10% of TAC, is being utilized). The application is limited to industrial/commercial fishers, and only for mono/single species case. Efforts to incorporate artisanal fishermen into the ITQ approach will likely add a fourth category of ITQs. Artisanal fishermen use small boats, take short trips, and stay close to shore.
	For standard fisheries, 100% of the TAC is auctioned in the first year the fishery goes into the ITQ system. 10% of the purchased license divests each year, hindering long-term control of the catch rights and facilitating more frequent market repricing of the rights. Single owners can not purchase more than 50% of the TAC either, to control market concentration. Owners can reassign portions of their quota they are not using for a particular year, also through the auction system. While international fishery interests may bid on ITQs, fish can only be landed by Chilean vessels. This effectively restricts market access to domestic fleets.
	Total TAC for fisheries under full exploitation is divided into long-term and annual licenses. The long-term licenses comprise 50% of TAC, last ten years, and were initially auctioned to the highest eligible bidder. Licenses depreciate 10% per year, with the capacity being reauctioned on an annual basis. This helps ensure long-term licenses expire gradually each year, and allows regular repricing. Single-year licenses comprise the remaining 50%, and are renewable, but only to established fisheries and to new comers. Public auctions of ITQs are limited to 5% of the TAC for that year. No single party can own more than 50% of the TAC.
	ITQ holders must accept the presence of scientific observers, and processing plants must provide information about the catch. In addition, all industrial fishing vessels regulated under any of the regimes must have a satellite global positioning system on board to allow the government to track vessel location.
	The ITQ usage remains experimental. More than 90% of the catch remains under the "Full Exploitation System," governed by standard command and control techniques. These include restricting access to fisheries to new agents, prohibitions on adding new fishing capacity, temporary or permanent closure of fishing areas, pre-set minimum sizes and weights for fish species, and gear restrictions. Catch quotas are also set for each vessel based on a percentage of historical catch levels. These are not transferable or divisible, and viewed as a transitory control mechanism until ITQs can be applied more broadly. Despite their usage for most of the annual catch, there is some evidence (Pena-Torres, 273) that they are ineffective.

Summary Analysis	
Efficacy of existing policy at solving problem	-Success of the programme is not clear. Current applications combined (black hake, orange roughly, squat lobster, and yellow prawn) make up only 1% of the total Chilean landings. While useful as a test of the ITQs, the affected sectors are far too small to affect overall fishery health at this point. -Final structuring of the ITQ policy seems to have protected Northern fishing interests, but reduced the potential benefits of the market-based quotas. For example, ITQs have thus far been applied to shrimp and cod fisheries, but not to the more heavily exploited pelagic fisheries more often under the full exploitation status. -Final structuring of the ITQ policy seems to have protected Northern fishing interests, but reduced the potential benefits of the market-based quotas. For example, ITQs have thus far been applied to shrimp and cod fisheries, but not to the more heavily exploited pelagic fisheries more often under the full exploitation status. -There have been some indications, especially in the hake fishery, of collusion among ITQ holders, as well as of weak monitoring and enforcement of the species. In the black hake fishery, quota prices are low and there is a suspicion that weak enforcement (allowing unregulated fishing) is the reason. -Enforcement remains a concern, though the number of violations has supposedly declined since ships were required to put GPS systems on vessels in 1999. However, use of an ITQ approach requires accurate and regularly-updated information on fishery health in order to accurately set TAC. Information in Chile is not considered reliable. On-board inspections are extremely limited. -Funds collected are remitted to the Treasury. While there is some indication this has increased funding support for fisheries oversight somewhat, this is not necessarily a permanent situation.
Rationale for success/failure	-Where ITQs are applied, fisheries do seem to have an improved incentive to manage fisheries for the long-term. Better management, and ability to time catch to highest market values, has increased returns to the fishermen. -Confidence in the efficacy is undermined somewhat by concerns that the TAC limits are not scientifically based and need improvement. -However, the small percentage of total catch currently covered suggests the ITQs are not yet addressing the broader goal of protecting Chilean fisheries. Exemptions for artisanal fishermen also need to be addressed. Open access to this sector may be one reason for an explosion in the number of vessels, with the sector growing 27% between 1994 and 1998. (Borregaard et al., 2001, p. 13).
Unanswered questions	-Impact of high market concentration on the ability of the ITQs to work. -Have the ITQs led to removal of capacity in the fishing fleet? -Cost of oversight is unknown.

Institutional Baseline Conditions in Country	
Legal	Constitution includes an article on the right of citizens to live in a clean environment, and this has been used to support many environmental law suits. The Environmental Framework Law also establishes a framework for responsibility for environmental damage (with burden of proof on the damaged). Property rights are enforced by the Constitution as well.
Fiscal and economic	Chile has functioning and generally observed tax, financial reporting/auditing, and insurance markets. There is even an insurance system that provides coverage for many environmental risks. Prices are relatively stable, and the level of taxation relatively low (10-40% for individuals, 30-40% for companies). Efforts are made to keep the tax system simple.
Government institutions	Most powers rest with the national (as opposed to regional) institutions. Provincial authorities are appointed by the head of government rather than elected. In general, there is no bribe taking. Institutions are encouraged to work together through the use of coordinating institutions (see below).
Environmental	The Environmental Framework Law provides the basic structure for environmental concerns in the country. The National Commission on Environment is a Coordinating Institution, not a Ministry. As such, it has extremely limited financial resources and its Director is considered a second-tier civil servant as compared to Ministers.

Detail on Policy Process	
History of response	Limited access to fisheries was first established in the 1960s in an effort to control the total allowable catch. In the 1970s, these policies came under criticism for preventing competition between potential investor groups during an era of high growth and widespread privatization. Law 2442 resulted, allowing free access to fisheries and accepting all fishing permit applications. Prior to the late 1980s, fishery laws were loosely defined and rarely enforced.
	In the late 1980s, a series of legal reforms were initiated to enforce more stringent quota policies for common-pool fish stocks. Authority for quotas fell under the regulatory body of SUBPESCA, and monitoring was assigned to SERNAP. However, these reforms failed due to insufficient information on the fisheries, and to conflict between affected groups and lobbying pressure from organized interest groups. Both regulatory instruments and fish stock monitoring were applied inconsistently. Furthermore, not enough was known about the behaviour of the fish stocks of concern to establish an appropriate TAC.
	The Merino Law of 1989 defined fisheries in full exploitation (e.g., the Northern and Southern Pelagic fisheries) from remaining ones with continuing free access. The Law sought to use transferable quotas as a replacement of to freezing a fleet's haul capacity as the method of choice to control catch. Challenged by Northern fishing firms concerned that the initial allocation of quotas would disadvantage them, portions of the Law were declared unconstitutional.
	The lack of standardized application of regulations frustrated private firms, and led to the establishment of seasonal closures (which were easy to apply to everybody) became the primary mechanism of fish stock regulation. Northern fishing companies lobbied successfully against subsequent efforts to enforce TACs, and each time succeeded in raising annual quotas, despite the lack of technical basis for what these quotas should be.
	The 1991 General Law of Fisheries and Aquaculture (FAGA) finally brought a stronger framework for curbing fish depletion. FAGA contained a mechanism to protect endangered fisheries by closing them entirely, for promoting underutilized fisheries, and for using ITQs as an allocation mechanism for fishing rights.
Evaluation of past success/failure	Regulatory efforts were applied inconsistently. Catch limits did not have a technical basis, and were successively increased due to industry lobbying alone. Enforcement was extremely weak, with not a single violator fined between 1982 and 1986.
Rationale for using EI	The failure of regulatory approaches to protect the fisheries spurred interest in economic instruments. There was no discussion of which instrument to choose: ITQs were chosen from the outset. The goal was to control access and overfishing by establishing transferable private fishing rights.
Legal basis for EI	The current ITQ policy is the result of the 1991 fisheries law. That law was a compromise between an earlier law under the military government based only on ITQs, and a more mixed approach (mix of instruments, differentiation of various social and cultural aspects of sub-populations, incorporate reality of weak enforcement capability) advocated by the democratic government.
	Zonal Fisheries Councils have some regulatory power under the Fisheries Law of 1991. However, the councils are comprised of representatives from different interest groups involved in the fishing industry (as opposed to environmental interests). Thus, the Council's objectives may not match the societal optimum.
Stakeholder involvement	There has not been wide support for, or consensus regarding, the introduction of ITQs. NGOs and the academic sector were mostly absent from the political debate around the fishery law in 1991. Lobbying efforts delayed the passage of the Merino law based on challenging the government's authority to limit access and sell property rights to fish stock. Explaining the benefits of the ITQ approach to various stakeholders has been a difficult and continuous process. Artisanal fishermen (small boats) opposed ITQs in general, fearing they would be outbid for rights by commercial enterprises and locked out of their profession.
Lead agencies	Subsecretary of Fishery (SUBPESCA) was a main party in developing the ITQs, defines broader fishery policies, and issues the annual catch quotas or calls for auction for ITQs. SERNAP (National Fishery Service) is the controlling authority, responsible for collecting data on the catches, landings, and boat registries. SERNAP is also in charge of enforcing national fishing regulations and inspecting fish quality and processing installations. The Chilean Navy monitors GPS data on vessel location. The National Commission of Environment has played virtually no role in the development or implementation of the fishery regulations, and is not represented on the fishery boards where decisions about catch quotas, resource policy, and regulations are made.

Key barriers addressed	
Detail on Policy Response	
Allocation of initial rights	The initial distribution of ITQs in the Pelagic fisheries was to be based on individual firms' percentage share of global catches in the previous three years. This created conflicts between the northern and southern fishing fleets, as it made it more difficult for the northern fishing industry to migrate southward. Finally, an allocation based on auctions was used.
On-going monitoring process	Monitoring and enforcement of SUBPECA and SERNAP have some additional funding and improved processes in recent years. However, sources suggest that the monitoring remains limited, making it difficult to confirm actual compliance with the quotas. Enforcement remains weak as well. Under the ITQ program, there have been only 100 infractions reported, and not a single resultant fine or conviction. Market monitoring is also weak: there is no central, transparent and efficient working public registry of transactions and their prices. This normally increases the risk of fraud.
Current successes	Some of the affected fisheries have undergone stock recoveries since the ITQs were implemented. Operators also say that they have been able to significantly improve the quality of their final products, and by better planning and operations, to re-build markets and diminish social conflict with their workers.
Remaining gaps/risks	Fisheries, especially in the North, remain highly concentrated: the largest group controls 55-65% of the total northern harvest, with the second group controlling 20-25%. This creates severe risks for lobbying and political interference that promotes the fishing interests over the long-term protection of the fisheries. In all markets, there are a relatively limited number of market participants. In the case of black hake, there have been no new entrants in over 8 years.
Source(s)	Compiled by Nicola Borregaard. Analysis based on McKee, C. 2001. A Review of the Individual Transferable Quotas (ITQ) in Fisheries; http://www.colby.edu/personal/t/thtieten/ch-fish.html and Nicola Borregaard, "ITQs in Chile - Moving from a Marginal System to a Key Policy Tool;" and Nicola Borregaard, Frank Convery, Paloma Gonzales, and Karen Gauer. Transferable Fishing Quotas In Chile - Case Study in the Design and Use of Market Based Instruments for Resource Policy (Draft), CIMPA, October 2001; Nicola Borregard, personal communication to Doug Koplow, February 2002.

Title	**Trade liberalization and environmental quality in rubber and cocoa plantations, Nigeria**
Country	Nigeria
Problem Definition	
Environmental impacts	Production of rubber and cocoa tends to occur in large plantations. Land is converted from diverse habitat to monoculture cropping.
Social impacts	Free trade was anticipated to increase the employment opportunities for domestic farmers, due to increased export-driven demand for their products. This was to provide a beneficial boost to the country as a whole by helping to diversify the employment base.
Solution Implemented	Trade liberalization was implemented broadly to help Nigeria increase the quality and responsiveness of its industrial sectors and to diversify the economic base. Trade policies were supported by successive devaluations of the Nigerian currency (making their exports more competitive in the world market) and some technical training.
Summary Analysis	
Efficacy of existing policy at solving problem	Trade liberalization does seem to have boosted exports in both the rubber and cocoa sectors, at least in the short term. The cocoa sector had many abandoned farms, so increased supply through farm rehabilitation rather than through new land conversions. This minimized the environmental impact of the change.
	In the case of rubber, two environmental problems arose. First, substantial new area was planted, with a net reduction in biodiversity. Second, farmers attempted to meet export demand by overtapping (slaughter tapping) the rubber trees. Many of these trees died, though country analysts point out that some of these were old and nearing the end of their productive life anyway. The tree deaths, however, did exacerbate soil erosion problems.
	During the structural adjustment period, usage of chemical fertilizers and fungicides rose sharply as well, contributing to environmental degradation. Usage dropped after the end of the structural adjustment period. This was due to falling prices for exports (as they had to be sold at true world prices), and to rising prices for the chemicals (as the Nigerian currency continued to devalue).
Rationale for success/failure	Liberalization did seem to increase demand for Nigerian crops, though the longer-term benefit on farm incomes was not discussed. -Had prices for rubber been more steady prior to trade liberalization, trees would have been replanted more regularly, avoiding the extent of tree deaths when prices and demand spiked. Similarly, because both oil and rubber came from the same Delta areas, high oil prices during the time of trade liberalization meant that farming was a secondary priority for residents. -While we do not have details on the elements of the structural adjustment policy, there are some indications that unrealistic crop prices during this period may have encouraged overcapacity during the transitional phases, as well as over reliance on chemical inputs. -While the case study sources do not attribute any environmental harm to rehabilitation of existing cocoa farms, one could argue that a transition back to wild ecosystems was reversed, and there were in fact losses here. -Sustainable management of the rubber sector did not arise.
Unanswered questions	-Could a different form of structural adjustment been implemented that forced more attention onto longer-term land management issues?
Institutional Baseline Conditions in Country	
Legal	Initial focus on the environment by the federal government came in the third National Development Plan of 1975-1980. The national framework law on environment in Nigeria came through the Federal Protection Decree No. 58 in 1988. This was amended by decree 59 in 1992 and further emphasized in the 1999 constitution. The law provides for the protection of Nigeria's environment and conservation of natural resources within the country, as well as making institutional and financial arrangements to support this goal. The law also provides both civil and criminal penalties for violators, and makes the offender liable for the cost of removal, reparation, restoration, restitution, and compensation.

Fiscal	Although there is wide latitude to implement a range of EIs (including pollution charges, marketable permits, subsidies, deposit systems, and enforcement incentives), the institutional base has generally not been strong enough to implement such policies. The exceptions are in some oil producing areas of Southern Nigeria.
Government institutions	The Federal Environmental Protection Agency (FEPA) was established in 1988. A Federal Ministry of the Environment was established by the civilian government in 1999 to police, coordinate, and collect data on environmental matters. The FEPA comprises the main part of this Ministry. There are 36 state-level environmental agencies. In addition, there are local authorities that address mainly urban waste collection and disposal. Most power resides at the federal level. Although FEPA must cooperate with lower levels of government, these lower levels do not have a clear mandate.
Environmental	As noted above, FEPA controls much of the environmental authority at the federal level, and the federal institutions drive environmental policy for the states and cities. FEPA was established in response to widespread dumping of radioactive wastes at Koko Port in Southern Nigeria in 1988. However, the agency policies do not cover many important environmental areas, such as agriculture and the use of agrochemical.

Detail on Policy Process

History of response	Trade liberalization was done quickly, with a structural adjustment period to cushion the shock of the changes.
Evaluation of past success/failure	Although the existing regulation seeks to discourage firms and individuals from causing pollution otherwise damaging the environment, it has had limited success. Environmental laws are not widely circulated; few of the populace have the will or the skills to bring suit for environmental damages; fines levied for environmental damages tend to be low; and government institutions lack skilled staff.
Rationale for using EI	To discourage environmental degradation from farming activities while concurrently earning increased revenues for the government.
Legal basis for EI	Existing provisions of the environmental decree provide adequate legal basis for implementing a range of economic instruments.
Stakeholder involvement	There was insufficient involvement and education of key stakeholders on the environmental impacts/issues associated with trade liberalization. The Licensed Buying Agents and the farmers both thought continuing with their existing farming practices would not be a problem.
Lead agencies	While a range of ministries (e.g., environment, agriculture, commerce) could play a role in training or enforcement, little has been done.
Key barriers addressed	Key barriers relating to education, technology transfer, and adoption of the polluter pays principle by key agencies remain mostly unaddressed.

Detail on Policy Response

Allocation of Initial rights	Markets were left to determine how much new supply to bring into the market and where this supply should be located.
On-going monitoring process	Low-level monitoring is taking place in the rural sector through tracking the usage of farm chemicals in crop production. Much more is needed.
Current successes	Economic objectives of increased farm incomes and improved social welfare for farms were met in the export crop sector. However, as observed in the case of rubber, this progress was achieved at a high environmental cost.
Remaining gaps/risks	Export-led growth in the natural resource sectors is likely to lead to increase land conversion, with concomitant environmental impacts. Countering this is the possibility that stabilizing farm incomes reduces urbanization pressures and enables workers to stop haphazard stripping of resources in an effort to survive.
Source(s)	UNEP, 5 November 2001. Economic Reforms, Trade Liberalization and the Environment: A Synthesis of UNEP Country Projects. Additional data provided by Okuneye, P.A., University of Agriculture, Abeokuta, Nigeria, May 2002 and March 2003.

Title	**Watershed protection fee for the Mount Makiling Forest Reserve, Philippines**
Country	Philippines
Problem Definition	
Environmental impacts	The Mt. Makiling Forest Reserve (MMFR) is a 4244 hectare forest reserve, owned by the government. It was placed under management control of the University of the Philippines Los Banos, to serve as a forest research laboratory to University students. Increasing in-migration for extractive use and habitation was posing and increasing threat to the reserve ecosystems and threatening the long-term health of the watershed. More than 300 households were occupied within the reserve, with more than 1,000 farmer claimants (including resident and non-resident).
Social impacts	Subsistence populations were treating the reserve as open access and seeking livelihood from the reserve's natural resources. Most were poor, and unlikely to move willingly.
Solution Implemented	The University has proceeded on two fronts. The first is to establish the claimants as a more stable group trained in sustainable practices. In addition to ensuring a longer-term interest in the reserve, the University hoped to use this group to help enforce sustainable behaviour and control additional settlement throughout the reserve. Efforts at formal accreditation have stalled due to opposition from one of the two main farming groups. This accreditation is viewed as granting secure property rights to existing farmers within the reserve, and hence has been a major stumbling block for the farmers.
	The second part of their strategy involves establishing fees to help protect the reserve. Unlike other reserves, MMFR receives no state funding, though it has received some funding from UNEP to structure the watershed pricing instrument. A recreational fee is already in place. New efforts to add a watershed protection fee are now underway; this fee would be levied on offsite users of MMFR resources, including residential, commercial, and institutional users. Fees will be added to water bills, or collected by the local government units (LGUs) for facilities not on the water grid. This fee has not been implemented due to a lack of legal basis at the current time. A third fee, essentially a rental payment by claimant farmers for using MMFR land, is also planned. The fee would provide credits for sustainable practices and increased penalties for damages. However, this fee has been deferred until a farmer accreditation programme is in place.
Summary Analysis	
Efficacy of existing policy at solving problem	Fee structure and enforcement will be important factors in whether the charge provides adequate funding for watershed management and rehabilitation, and provides proper incentives to users for sustainable behaviour.
	While legal barriers have impeded adoption of any fee in the MMFR, other watersheds do have this authority if they are protected areas under the National Integrated Protected Areas act. Some of these are evaluating the use of watershed protection fees as well, and may face fewer barriers.
	The desire to charge farmers for using the land is logical. However, the current delay of all watershed protection activities for this group until they are given formal property rights is likely to greatly impede appropriate behaviour by this group. They may delay resolution of the accreditation issue in order to avoid the costs they will incur subsequently.
Rationale for success/failurea	Lack of legal authority on collecting funds, coupled with an absence of a clear mandate from university management and the fact that other university staff need to figure out the implementation plan in their spare time have all delayed the implementation of an important EI to protect the watershed. This greatly reduces the University's bargaining power to achieve a sustainable solution in a reasonable time frame.
	-The provision of many services and benefits to the claimants is likely to increase migration into the reserve, the opposite of what the University hopes will occur. Furthermore, the University does not seem to have used its power of eviction to ensure that existing claimants utilize sustainable practices even before a formal accreditation programme has been implemented.
	-Proposed charges for off-site users appear to be a flat rate, and quite low. This may not accurately reflect the actual costs these users put on the watershed.

Unanswered questions	-Fee levels and cost sharing between the University, the National Water Resources Board and the local government have yet to be worked out. -Fee structure, levels, and differentiation by user class are not clear, but can have important incentive effects on various groups. -Why has the university management not taken a more active role? Are there political considerations not being addressed that may undermine the charge scheme at a later point? -Even with sustainable management of the resources, to what extent will use of the land for agriculture compromise site biodiversity?

Institutional Baseline Conditions in Country

Legal	
Fiscal	
Government institutions	
Environmental	

Detail on Policy Process

History of response	Influx of residents into the MMFR has been a recurring problem for decades. In the 1970s, the University's approach was simply to evict them. Current efforts focus on co-partnership with the residents to protect the forest. The University has a special unit addressing community issues, including technical assistance in agroforestry systems, limited distribution of fruit seedlings, some vocational scholarships for children of the farmers, and provision of some health care services. There has also been an effort to develop an accreditation programme for farmers regarding the sustainability of their practices. University policy towards the settlers has been ad hoc; no formal positions by top management have been established. This vacuum has led farmer groups to be more active in making demands on the university, an initiative supported by an external NGO.
Evaluation of past success/failure	Eviction policies did not work, since people (whether the same or different) kept coming back. The situation appears still to be one of open access, though there may be de facto claims in place by the existing population that helps to curtail new intrusions. Some cooperative approach was clearly needed in order to achieve sustainable management of the reserve with little or no budget. However, the establishment and enforcement of these management norms has been very slow in coming, and some farm and industry groups may benefit financially from further delays.
Rationale for using EI	UNEP coordination with University staff led to the conclusion that some type of EI made sense, since funds were needed to run the reserve and many parties were benefiting from its services. The research group focused on each resource area: farmers, outside beneficiaries, recreational users, and hikers, and came up with a charge for each. No alternative instruments were discussed.
Legal basis for EI	The University has a clear legal basis to manage the resource and impose fees for accessing the resources within MMFR. Charging a watershed protection fee to facilities outside the reserve is not as clear cut. In addition, the collection mechanism for the fee is the facility's water bill, creating the impression that MMFR is charging for water itself. The rationale is that the forest reserve and integrated watershed are a core input to the provision of high quality water to off-site users. However, confusion remains, and a clear legal basis does not yet exist. The University is working with the National Water Resources Board and local water districts to develop a memorandum of understanding, as these institutions have the legal mandate to collect any payments that may be established. While most of the water districts have signaled their willingness to reach some agreement like this, University officials recognize that the ultimate agreements may be weak and not all districts will be willing to collect and share these revenues with them.
Stakeholder involvement	Public meetings were held to discuss the proposed fee and its rationale. These were initiated and led by the university. These involved resort owners, water district representatives, and institutional water consumers. Meetings with individual groups of water users were also held at the University. Resort owners are organized and expressed general support to the watershed protection project. They are willing to contribute in-kind by employing members of the upland community in their resorts, viewing them as a substitute for cash outlays.

	Farming communities are organized into two main groups, which are now federated. They were notified that they would be expected to contribute to watershed protection, but that this contribution would be in-kind. In-kind contributions discussed included participation in forest protection initiatives and/or adoption of sustainable farming practices. Essentially, they are being required to adopt more sustainable practices in order to retain their access to subsidized resources. These discussions were suspended until an accreditation scheme is in place, allowing existing practices to continue until a future date.
Lead agencies	University, National Water Resources Board, local water districts.
Key barriers addressed	

Detail on Policy Response

Allocation of initial rights	Rights to forest services were granted to the University, but have heavily utilized by farmers and others moving into the reserve. Water users outside the reserve also benefit from the water purification services that the watershed provides. To more equitably distribute the costs of providing these services, the College of Forestry and Natural Resources evaluated appropriate charge schemes. They calculated a simple average cost of providing water to users by dividing the cost of watershed protection by the cubic meters of water consumed by each group. Initial fees are set at about PhP15.60/month for an average household. This is in line with survey results on how much these citizens are willing to pay (about PhP 36/month per household).
On-going monitoring process	Property rights regimes have not been finalized. Water charges will be linked to water consumption with, for most users, is already metered. Not clear how monitoring of sustainable practices of farmers will be evaluated.
Current successes	Philosophical agreement with the approach by most parties.
Remaining gaps/risks	-Actually setting and implementing the charges has yet to occur. -Clear and accurate valuation process for in-kind contributors remains to be developed.
Source(s)	Compiled by Herminia Francisco, 2002.

Title	Trade liberalization, bananas and environmental quality in Ecuador
Country	Ecuador
Problem Definition	
Environmental impacts	Banana production provides jobs and export earnings, but land conversion to increase banana production affected soil health and biodiversity. Pesticide use also caused health problems for workers.
Social impacts	Social impacts from trade liberalization included the potential increase in jobs in the sector, the displacement of people from subsistence agriculture, and the conversion of manual-intensive to technology-intensive production in the farm sector, potentially yielding job loss and increased chemical exposure.
Solution Implemented	Trade liberalization was undertaken concurrently with currency devaluations to promote agricultural exports. Export price guarantees and credit subsidies further promoted increased production. Only much later were regulatory controls introduced to curb environmental and worker health problems associated with the rapid growth in banana production.
Summary Analysis	
Efficacy of existing policy at solving problem	The policy packages did a good job increasing banana production. Yield, area under production, and total production all grew rapidly during the period. Environmental considerations were secondary, and not integrated into the planning process from the outset. While regulatory controls during the 1990s have slowed expansion and reduced chemical exposure for workers, these policies could have been implemented at the outset of the export promotion plan. In addition, government efforts at trade liberalization were supported by domestic credit subsidies and price guarantees, creating an artificially buoyant spur to increase production, bringing with it a host of environmental problems.
Rationale for success/failure	The programme was perhaps an export success, but more careful attention to the environmental and human health aspects of rapid growth in agricultural exports could have generated more sustainable (both environmentally and economically) job growth.
Unanswered questions	-As banana production has come under more free trade, how has the sector faired? -How effective have the regulatory efforts to protect human health and the environment been? -Did the government ever consider restricting access to price guarantees and credit subsidies only to farms who used sustainable production techniques?
Institutional Baseline Conditions in Country	
Legal	
Fiscal	
Government institutions	
Environmental	
Detail on Policy Process	
History of response	During 1980-89, periodic (though small) devaluation of the Ecuadorian currency, coupled with periodic adjustments to the exchange rate, made the country's exports more cost effective. Coupled with generally falling interest rates, rationalization of credit to productive industry, and direct credit subsidies to the agricultural sector, domestic production and export of bananas increased. It is not clear from available information whether the devaluations were an integral part of an export promotion plan, or due to other macroeconomic forces. While the impact of these policies on deforestation cannot be estimated with precision, it is clearly a significant factor. Since the mid-1980s, timber extraction and the unrestricted planting of agricultural products (including bananas) has been the largest source of deforestation in the country.

	Attempts to introduce new varieties of bananas in the 1980s to increase land productivity (and reduce the hectares needed under production) did not work out as planned. Rather, the returns to banana producers increased during the period due to guaranteed minimum export prices. Rapidly rising costs of inputs to banana production eroded most of the profit, however, and many small producers often ran losses.
	During 1990-1994, import restrictions were replaced by import duties, allowing more cost efficient importation of productivity-enhancing capital equipment. This led to a growth in banana plantations at an average rate of 18%, much higher than in the previous decade. Losses in habitat and biodiversity were substantial. This was encouraged through continued protection for growers from world prices, through required minimum prices to producers set by the government. Fixed band exchange rates also buffered declines in the value of domestic currency, preventing price spikes in imported equipment.
	During 1995-1999, fiscal and monetary reforms were introduced. A number of trade agreements were also made, improving market access for banana exports. Between 1994 and 1999, regulatory programs to address environmental, worker health, and crop diversification issues in the banana sector were addressed, slowing the expansion of area under banana cultivation. Banana yields have risen due to application of technology and better plantation management. Despite price guarantees for banana sales, profits rose only for larger, more technically-advanced plantations (with lower costs). Small and medium producers remained unprofitable. Environmental performance has generally been better at the larger, more technically-advanced farms.
Evaluation of past success/failure	Policies have been fairly consistent during the period: cheap credit and price guarantees, along with efforts to increase access to export markets. The failure of these approaches from an environmental perspective is visible through the enactment of the Environmental Security Regulations for the Banana Sector, the Plant Quarantine Handbook and the Export Facilitation Law, all in 1994. These addressed norms for pest control, packaging, and re-conversion of plantations. In 1995, norms regarding crop diversification were passed. It was not until 1998 that the Plant Health Regulations were passed, and 1999 that brought the Environmental Management Law. These lagged the introduction of export promotion activities by almost 20 years.
Rationale for using EI	Trade liberalization was a broad scale way to boost sales of Ecuadorian products abroad. This objective was pursued using economic subsidy policies, though with little regard to impacts of this growth on worker health or safety.
Legal basis for EI	Not known.
Stakeholder involvement	Not known.
Lead agencies	
Key barriers addressed	
Detail on Policy Response	
Allocation of initial rights	
On-going monitoring process	
Current successes	
Remaining gaps/risks	
Source(s)	UNEP Synthesis Report, 2001.

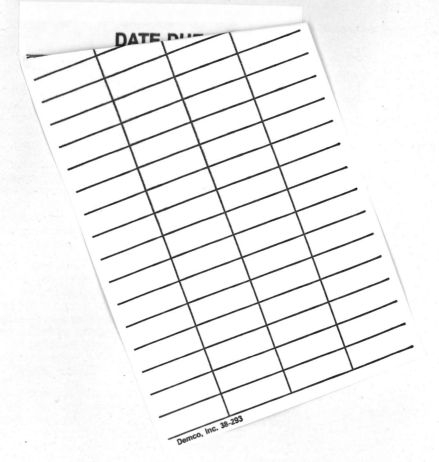

DATE DUE

Demco, Inc. 38-293